FISHING THE EDGE

FISHING THE EDGE

Techniques and Tales from
Surf, Boat, and Kayak

By John Skinner

©2022. FISHING THE EDGE
Techniques and Tales from Surf, Boat, and Kayak

Printed And Distributed by On the Edge Communications Inc.

All Book Rights Reserved by John Skinner

All rights reserved. No part of this book may be reproduced or utilized in any form or means, electrical or mechanical, including photocopying or recording, or by information storage and retrieval systems without written permission of the publisher, ON THE EDGE COMMUNICATIONS INC.

Printed in the United States of America

ON THE EDGE COMMUNICATIONS INC.
GREENPORT, NY 11944

ISBN 978-0-9906914-3-3

Design and Layout: Stacey Kruk-Damiano
www.skgraphics.net

Cover Design: Stacey Kruk-Damiano

Front/Back Cover Photos by Bill Moulton
www.bfantastic.com
Instagram: @bfantasticalltheway

Other Books by the Author
FISHING FOR SUMMER FLOUNDER
STRIPER PURSUIT
FISHING THE BUCKTAIL
A SEASON ON THE EDGE

DEDICATION

Dedicated to my wife Kim. My best catch by far.

ACKNOWLEDGMENTS

Thanks go out to my brother, Captain Bob Skinner, his wife, Marie, and Captain John Halkias for editing the manuscript. Bob's and John's perspectives as fishermen with editors' eyes and Marie's vantage point as an avid reader of a wide range of subjects combined to provide valuable guidance. My daughter, Katie, went through the manuscript with an amazing eye for every little detail. I sleep well at night knowing a Princeton graduate has proofread my manuscript. Time spent fishing good water is the foundation of a project like this, and I thank Halkias, Rick Kohut, John "Doc" Keriazes, and John Sweeney for taking me fishing on their boats to some of the finest fishing grounds in the Northeast. Finally, thanks to Zeno Hromin of *The Surfcasters Journal* for his selfless assistance and priceless advice with the publishing details required to make this book a reality.

TABLE OF CONTENTS

CHAPTERS

1. INTRODUCTION 1
2. WEAKFISH THEN AND NOW 3
3. BEACH BLACKFISH ON JIGS 15
4. BLACKFISH JIGGING FROM BOAT AND KAYAK 25
5. MY FIRST KAYAK 39
6. KAYAK UPGRADE 49
7. FINDING A HONEY HOLE 57
8. THE PEDAL KAYAK 65
9. ADAPTING TO A NEW FISHERY 69
10. GAME CHANGER 77
11. ELECTRIFIED 85
12. EPIC BATTLE 95
13. SPRING FLATS BLUEFISH SCARE 105
14. ALBIE EXPLOSION 113
15. SPOOKED 127
16. SHARK! 137
17. SEA BASS JIGGING 151
18. PORGY JIGGING 157
19. THE CREW 161
20. OCEAN FLUKE 169
21. BIG SPOONS – BIG BASS 181
22. MY 50 YEARS ON THE EDGE
    AND SOME PARTING ADVICE 189

CHAPTER 1
INTRODUCTION

"Bump." It's that feeling on the end of the rod that signals the start of something special. The possibilities are endless. Even when we think we know what will follow, we are often surprised by an outsized fish or an unexpected species. For serious anglers, the feeling never gets old. For many new anglers, the bump becomes a gateway drug to a lifetime addiction, but a good one. I should know, as it's been more than fifty years since that first fish bumped my rod, igniting a passion that has lasted through and often guided my life. The obsession that started for me in Northeast waters now includes the Florida fisheries, as I move back and forth following the fishing seasons.

I'm asked often what my favorite fish is. I think the answer is that it's the one closest to my line. That's part of my motivation for this project. I've previously written very in-depth books focused almost solely on striped bass and summer flounder (fluke), yet for much of my life I've pursued other species such as weakfish, false albacore, bluefish, blackfish, sea bass, and even porgies with equal intensity. Half of my year is now spent chasing redfish, snook, sea trout, and tarpon in Florida. While the bump of an unseen fish on the end of the line might elevate an angler's pulse, the sight of a shallow water redfish coming up behind a lure can stop one's heart. What I've learned in making the seasonal transitions between Northern and Southern fishing goes beyond technique, as it's clear that what you learn in one fishery is very likely to apply to entirely different far-away fish. Some of my best Florida fishing has come from thinking like a Northern striper fisherman.

It all starts with techniques and strategies, and they will form the foundation of this book. There are serious chapters on striped bass and fluke fishing, but I direct the reader to my previous books for more thorough treatments of those subjects. The primary focus here will be on the many other species that I fish for. As is the case with my *Striper Pursuit* and *Fishing for Summer Flounder* books, you'll find little square barcodes, called *QR Codes*, placed strategically throughout this book. Scan one of these with a tablet or smartphone and it will take you to the video support for the part of the book you're reading. A reader without Internet access will find the information given in these pages complete and thorough without viewing the videos, while the combination of what is written and the free video support will be both enlightening and entertaining.

The tools of fishing have evolved tremendously in my fifty years as an angler, and the productive application of today's gear is covered in detail in these pages. This is especially true in the chapters that involve kayak fishing. Because I've watched fisheries rise and fall, only to rise again, I'll also dig back into the decades past for timeless approaches that remain relevant.

Finally, there are special times in fishing when that bump on the end of the line turns into an extraordinary battle that's remembered for a lifetime. I'll share my most intense experiences here, all while integrating the techniques and strategies that made it happen. There's a lot to cover, and there's a school-skipping teenager headed out early on a spring morning to catch the tide and the fish it will bring. Let's go.

CHAPTER 2
WEAKFISH THEN AND NOW

My high school senior skip day began at dawn as I drove east to Long Island's South Fork with some fishing tackle, a 1963 10 hp outboard, and a full 6-gallon gas tank in the trunk of my 1967 Mercury Monterey. This was 1979, and the spring Peconic Bay weakfish fishery was on fire. I was scheduled to meet up with two classmates, Jim and Kevin, who lived on the South Fork and were avid fishermen. We had schemed about this day for weeks. Kevin had an old 15-ft wood boat in Southampton, but its 9.5 hp motor would be insufficient to push the three of us to the weakfish grounds off Cow Neck. Our solution was to turn his boat into a *twin screw* for the day. The transom was wide enough for two motors, so we mounted my 10 hp and the more modern and lower-profile 9.5 hp next to each other. They fit – barely. With a 6-gallon gas can for each motor, we would have speed and range. There were no electronics, nor were they needed. The unconventional scheme was the product of many lunch-time discussions. My parents sanctioned the trip, understanding that it was probably better that I was out fishing instead of partying on a beach in The Hamptons, which was the other option for the day.

We learned quickly that it's not easy to control a boat with two independent outboards, as we bounced off a bulkhead before making it out of the first creek when Kevin turned one of the throttles the wrong way momentarily and then overcompensated. With no damage done, we proceeded a little more carefully and were soon on the open water of Peconic Bay. With nothing left to hit, Kevin opened up both throttles and pointed us toward the ¾-mile-wide stretch of water between the south tip of Robins Island and Cow Neck, known as the South Race. This sometimes-treacherous channel funnels water between Little Peconic Bay to the east and Great Peconic Bay to the west. Many things could have gone wrong this day, but they all went right, starting with the weather. It was a beautiful calm day as we approached the small fleet drifting with the incoming current.

Kevin and I started with the standard of the time, a 1/2-ounce ball-head jig with a 9-inch strawberry Mann's Jelly Worm tipped with a strip of squid. Jim claimed to have a secret weapon – a Burke Jig-A-Do head to carry the Jelly Worm. When you dragged this through the water it made the worm wiggle. He told me about this ahead of time, so I also had a few with me. My rod was a 2-piece honey-colored 7-footer that I bought at Morsan's paired with a Penn 720 spooled with 12-pound-test monofilament. Jim was proud of his 6-foot Altenkirch custom rod that he had won in a fishing contest.

Roughly 15 scattered boats, including the *Brand X* party boat out of Greenport, made up the fleet drifting in about 25 feet of water as we settled in for the first drift. I cast up-current, left the bail open until I knew the jig was on the bottom, then closed the bail and began a slow jigging action while turning the reel handle slowly. After his jig hit bottom, Jim began a very slow retrieve on his Jig-A-Do lure to get the worm wiggling. He was hit almost immediately, and I wasn't far behind and we soon had a pair of 8-pounders in the boat. I'm not sure we thought through what we were going to do with the fish, but one of the other two had the bright idea that we could make a stringer out of the boat's anchor line, and keep the fish in the cold early-season water on the 20+-minute drifts. We did not have a cooler.

Drift after drift produced bent rods and weakfish in the 6- to 9-pound class. Jim was doing a little better with the Jig-A-Do, which is a lead head with a plastic collar on it that makes it wiggle when you drag it through the water. I switched over to that and was able to match Jim's catch, with Kevin not far behind. As time went by, the fish stringer grew to the point that it took two of us to haul it over the side at the end of each drift. At one point when we drifted near the party boat and the anglers with their higher vantage point caught a look at the 20-foot stringer of weakfish, they were highly entertained to say the least. For our age, we were actually pretty good fishermen and were doing quite well in relation to others in the fleet. At one point at the top of a drift another boat set-up almost on top of us and Jim just looked at them and said "Go away! We're catching fish here!" and they did just that as we laughed like the high school kids we were.

When the current slowed, so did the fishing. Of course, we had some sort of a competition going. Jim was a fish ahead of me when I pulled out a mackerel green sinking Rebel. Both Jim and Kevin thought it was a dumb choice, but I read in *The Fisherman Magazine* that weakfish loved it, so I brought it with me. The plug took a little time to find the bottom, then I engaged a slow retrieve. They stopped laughing at the plug when that first cast produced our biggest fish of the day, a 9 ½-pounder. I got one more after that to pass Jim, but then the current died completely and the wind started coming up, so we headed for the dock with a boat-load of weakfish. More precisely, 23 weakfish. This was at a time when there wasn't a lot of catch-and-release happening, and the nuns had taught us lots of stuff about being good to other people but apparently not much about conservation. Despite not having a cooler or ice, we managed to get those fish to a seafood market in good enough condition that they actually bought them for 35 cents a pound. A good chunk of that money was then spent on Rolling Rock beer.

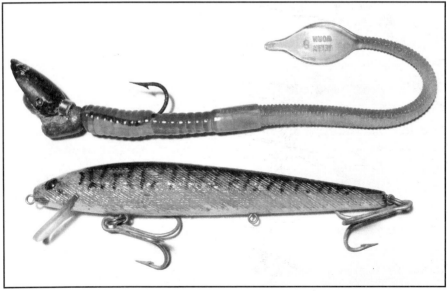

A 9-inch Mann's JellyWorm on a Burke Jig-A-Do head and the actual sinking Rebel that caught on the Skip Day trip.

The great fishing in the Peconics and other parts of the Northeast kept up for a few more years, including a phenomenal run on the Long Island Sound beaches in 1981. By the late 80's, the fishery had collapsed. Perhaps the best measure of the East End weakfish population was the weigh-in list of the annual Peconic Bay Weakfish Tournament. The Riverhead Sportsmen's Club held the weekend-long tournament during the middle of May to coincide with the peak of the Peconic Bay weakfish run. In 1994, only one weakfish, a 7.82-pounder was caught during the contest. The following year was not much better with four weakfish entered. The largest of those weighed only 3.25 pounds. None of the seven fish entered in the 1996 contest broke the 3-pound mark. Given those dismal results, it seemed almost miraculous that many weaks were caught in the 2000 contest, and the top ten fish weighed between 8.44 and 9.64 pounds.

My kids, Katie and Mikey, and I made a tradition out of fishing that contest from my 16-foot Starcraft. We usually did very well working the Rose Grove and Robins Island areas with diamond jigs and 4-inch Storm Wildeyes. The highlight of our efforts was an hour-long binge of big tiderunners in the 2001 contest that produced an 11.6-pounder for Katie that easily won the children's division and would have placed second in the adult division had she been old enough. The next 20 years were generally pretty tough for weakfish on Long Island, with few bright spots such as the 2020 summer fishing in Great South Bay. Most summers you could catch good numbers of weakfish in the Peconics, but these were almost all small fish in the 12- to 18-inch range.

Why these seemingly large numbers of summer weaks were not surviving long enough to generate good fishing with spring tiderunners remains somewhat of a mystery. An article in the April 2021 issue of *On the Water Magazine* detailed acoustic tag research results that suggested that the vast majority of weakfish were not surviving through the winter, primarily due to predation, especially from Bottlenose Dolphin. In the study, weakfish were implanted with acoustic tags that ping a large array of listening stations up and down the coast. The article stated that of 149 weakfish tags deployed in the fall, only 2 pinged off listening stations the following spring. The same article went on to say that necropsies on stranded dolphins show that 49% of their winter diet is weakfish. While this is just one study, it does suggest a reason why the large number of

Mikey and Katie with Junior Division winning fish in the 2003 Peconic Bay Weakfish Tournament.

small summer weakfish in the Peconics didn't return in good numbers in subsequent years – until May of 2021.

It was supposed to be a mixed bag trip. There were bass and blues at Jessup's Neck and fluke at the Greenlawns, but I would start by looking for some weakfish in Noyack. I would never make it to the other fishing. I was immediately encouraged as I cruised the boat over my Noyack weakfish GPS marks in about 40 feet of water and saw more fish on the fishfinder than I did on my previous visit. My go-to offering in this spot is based on the same 30-pound-test leader rig that I use for fluke, with a Surgeons Loop at the bottom and a dropper loop a foot above that. On this morning the bottom loop had a 1-ounce bucktail tipped with squid, and the dropper loop had a plain 3/0 Gamakatsu Baitholder hook with a 4-inch Gulp Grub and squid strip. I rarely use bait of any kind, but the weakfish fishing had been so tough over the preceding 20 years that I was willing to make an exception to give myself the best chance of catching them. My presentation is simple. Drop the rig to the bottom and give easy sweeps upward with the rod. If I start losing contact with the bottom, then I flip the bail and let out enough line to hit the bottom again. I use 7-foot medium action spinning rods with 2000 or 3000 size reels spooled with 10- or 15-pound-test braided line.

Despite the good marks on the fishfinder, 20 minutes passed without a fish. I proceeded toward a second set of GPS marks less than a half-mile away, but decided to cruise there slow enough that I could watch the fishfinder for schools of fish along the way. Weakfish have large swim bladders that give off strong echoes on sonar, so they show up easily on a fishfinder. Approximately half-way to my intended second spot, I saw enough on the fishfinder to stop and drop the rig.

It took about a minute to hook the first weakfish, which at around 16 inches would be the smallest of the trip. The jig didn't make it to the bottom on the next drop as another weakfish grabbed it. The marks on the fishfinder were becoming more concentrated. I caught another fish as soon as the jig went down, followed by a double-header. I decided to skip the squid strips and go with only Gulp grubs on the bucktail and teaser hook. One of my first drops with that was intercepted by a double header of weakfish before it hit the bottom. I was done using squid for the rest of the trip. This would go on for the rest of this drift, which lasted 40 minutes and produced 23 weakfish. The fish were all in the 3- to 5-pound range, except for one a little bigger at around 6 pounds and the initial 16-incher. I only lost the school of fish because I drifted up a ledge and out of the productive depth. At a drift speed that was steady between 0.5 and 0.6 mph, I had just drifted over a third of a mile while constantly on fish that were stacked so thick that it was uncommon for my jig to make it to the bottom.

I was on dead-quiet water with the nearest boat well over a mile away. Concerned about spooking the massive school, I deployed the trolling motor and ran right up my drift line on my plotter. I somehow manage to miss the school doing this, and even after finally using the outboard, it took me 40 minutes to get back on the fish. This drift would turn out to be even better than the previous. It lasted 32 minutes and produced 25 fish. I think I was able to catch a couple of more fish in less time because I was no longer wasting time cutting squid. I started a third drift and caught a few fish, but lost the current and the bite. The last fish I caught was the largest at somewhere over 7 pounds. In total I boated 52 weakfish.

The largest of 52 weakfish bucktailed in Peconic Bay on a May 2021 trip.

I got back to the spot a few days later on a friend's boat. We caught fish, but nothing like the action I had, as the schools were more scattered. We eventually moved a mile away to a deeper area of 60 feet of water and found the fish stacked thick and hitting diamond jigs. That set the stage for a few days later when I brought my daughter Katie with me.

Kids grow up, stuff happens, opportunities arise, and soon the fishing trips that used to happen every weekend when they were young happen once a year if you're lucky. With Katie now seven years beyond her Princeton days and working as an Assistant Professor in Robotics, this was the first time I would have a chance to fish with her in a couple of years. It was a gray and breezy day, but the sheltered Peconics provided an acceptable comfort level after making the 6-mile ride from Greenport.

There were only two boats in the general area upon our arrival, giving us plenty of room to find a pile of fish to have to ourselves. With 60 feet of water and the wind blowing against the current, I set her up with a plain 3-ounce diamond jig with a 4-inch Gulp teaser above it. After shutting down on what the fishfinder showed was a stack of fish, I told her to drop to the bottom and just bounce the jig up and down once it got there. Her rod was arched over before I could put a Gulp on my hook, as a 5-pound weakfish grabbed her jig before it hit the bottom.

The fish were stacked even higher than they were on the bucktail trip in the other spot. We drifted off the school in a couple of minutes, so the next time I motored over them I deployed the trolling motor and turned on its *Spot Lock* feature to hold the boat over the school. Spot Lock uses GPS positioning and will continuously adjust power and direction in order to electronically anchor the craft in place. I wouldn't have "anchored" if it was crowded, because I wouldn't want to interfere with the drifting boats. Now there was only one other boat in the area, and he was almost a half-mile away. The second boat that had been nearby was a commercial boat that left, likely filling his 100-pound trip limit. For the next two hours we spot-locked on stacks of weakfish and dropped metal on them. Despite losing a couple of rigs to bluefish, we totaled 46 weakfish in 2.5 hours of fishing. It was great to hear her say "My arms are getting tired!" as she hauled one of several double-headers to the boat. Her best was a beautiful 8-pounder that reminded me of the great 1970s fishery.

Katie with a big weak caught diamond jigging in Peconic Bay, 2021.

Several times while we were fishing, I dropped an underwater camera to the bottom. I knew the visibility wasn't great, but because I had previously been able to record good underwater porgy video a couple of miles west, I thought maybe the water would be clear enough to observe the immense schools of weaks. When I got home and reviewed the video, I was encouraged at the start because there seemed to be adequate visibility at the surface. However, as the camera descended, the video became darker and darker until it was pitch black well before it reached the bottom. The video at the bottom was completely black as the camera was not able to record any light at all. This was unexpected. This was 60 feet of water but I had recorded beautiful video with the same camera in 85 feet off Montauk. From what I could see on the video, this turbid water was filtering out all of the light. I'm aware that cameras have a dynamic range that might prevent them from seeing very faint light, but even if I allowed for this, it was still mighty dark down there and I doubt anyone knew it! I was taking such great care to keep my diamond jigs nice and shiny, even washing the used ones in fresh water and wiping them dry so that they could maintain their shine. What were the fish actually seeing? What lure might stand out best? I immediately devised a test.

I had done enough surfcasting and boat fishing for stripers at night to know that dark-colored bucktails often out-produced white after dark. My favorite night bucktail color is wine-red, but I would pick black as a close second. Since these fish were living in darkness, would a black diamond jig out-produce the chrome that everyone was using? I even took notice to see that the commercial fishermen were also using chrome. None of this was too surprising, as it's hard to find any color besides chrome when buying diamond jigs.

In rummaging through beat-up old diamond jigs to paint black, I came across a single glow diamond jig made by Marathon Lures. I added that to the test as well. I gave my brother Bob a call and told him I needed help with an experiment, and he was happy to join me for a jigging test. He's a fine fisherman and could yo-yo a jig just as well as I could, so this would be an easy comparison. I rigged identical rods the same way with the only difference being jig color, and off we went to the jigging grounds.

This was a very strong run, as we had no trouble finding a fish pile to get started on when we arrived. By now I was aware that a couple of other boats were also spot-locking on the fish, or using their engines to lock onto the schools, so I didn't hesitate to spot-lock whenever I found fish. There weren't many boats on these grounds on a weekday anyway, likely because there were porgies, fluke, bass, and blues in other parts of the bay to fish for as well.

We put black up against chrome to start, and traded rods frequently to make sure that fishing technique didn't skew the results. After more than two hours of fishing, it became abundantly clear that black was out-fishing chrome. It wasn't even close. With plenty of tide left and lots of fish to work on, I tied on the glow jig to see how it would do against black. Glow out-fished black easily. We quit after catching a total of 61 weakfish. Although the majority were caught on the Gulp teaser, I did not want to do away with the teaser because I knew it would help us catch and locate feeding fish. More than enough hit the metal for us to make a good comparison. I did two underwater camera drops to confirm that the near-bottom water beneath us was indeed dark. When I got home, I reviewed all of the trip video to accurately tabulate the results. They were stunning.

When considering weakfish only, the chrome jig caught only one, the black jig caught six, and the glow jig caught eight. The remarkable thing about the productivity of the glow jig was that we only started using it when we saw how badly black was beating chrome, so glow was used only about half as long as either black or chrome, yet it caught more than the other colors combined!

Equally amazing was the count of foul-hooked fish. Besides the 61 mouth-hooked weaks that we boated, we foul-hooked nine. One was on black, one on glow, and seven on chrome! Not only could the weakfish apparently not see the chrome jig well enough to eat it, they couldn't detect it well enough to get out of its way!

I'll take a stab at explaining the results. The effectiveness of the glow jig in darkness is obvious. It gives off light and stands out. Black vs. chrome is more interesting. My son Michael had a quick explanation that I can't beat. The shiny jig in the absence of significant light will mirror its surroundings and blend in. The black jig will have the best chance at producing a noticeable silhouette in near-darkness. This makes sense to me, which gives me further confidence in our observations. Looking ahead, there's going to be a little more black and a little less silver in my lure arsenal for low light fishing. I always thought silver was natural and could never be wrong. I've changed my mind about this. Prey definitely would rather blend in and be invisible than stand out and be targeted by a predator. Maybe the fact that so many bait fish are silver is a product of natural selection because they blend in and are harder to see.

My video observation that those big schools of Peconic Bay weakfish were living in darkness brought up other things besides lure color. The part of Peconic Bay where I did this test is strange in that there is what I can only describe as species segregation. Beginning just west of Jessup's Neck is *the porgy spot*. The porgy fishing is so good there that party boats move to the North Fork for the month of May to get in on it, and I even see a Connecticut party boat that makes the trip daily. I'll detail that fishing in Chapter 18. I've recorded underwater video in 40 feet there, and it's fine. I can see all of the fish interested in my chum pot. Moving northeast about a half a mile is the Jessup's rip. It sometimes has stripers, but it's often so loaded with medium to large bluefish that you can't get at the bass without sacrificing gear bitten off by the blues. A few minutes northeast of that is the weakfish jigging spot. There is another weakfish spot a few minutes east of that. Greenlawns, the well-known fluke spot, is a few minutes north of the first weakfish spot.

There is some mixing, but those two weakfish spots that are near 60-70 feet of water hold predominantly weakfish. I have video-checked these and both have darkness near the bottom. Is it possible that the weakfish congregate in these two spots because they can use the 24 hours of near-darkness to avoid being eaten by bluefish? I bet that's the case, since reeling up a weakfish that has been chopped by a bluefish is not at all uncommon. I've seen this segregation play out in surf fishing also. I know a stretch of bay shoreline that is awesome for big bluefish, but I've never caught a bass there. It's not that there are no bass in the area, as I can walk to a great bass spot from the bluefish spot. I'll write about a scary incident on the bluefish spot in Chapter 13. Keep in mind when you're fishing that these segregations occur. In particular if you're hunting weakfish, avoid blues. Stripers are more tolerant of them, but schoolies likely avoid big choppers.

Finally, trip-planning for jigging the Peconic Bay weaks was tide-related. Although it's always nice to start early in the morning, we had great bites in the middle of the day under a bright sun. While talking to a long-time Greenport charter captain about the weakfish run he reminded me how back in the 70's and early 80's the best weakfish action was almost always at dawn or dusk, or after dark if you fished then. Unfortunately, the water clarity in the Peconics has diminished over the years. It sounds reasonable to me that because the main weakfish schools are swimming in constant darkness these days, they don't care much about how much sunlight there is.

Time will tell what the future holds for weakfishing in the Northeast and mid-Atlantic waters, but the observation of the Peconic fishery is likely to translate across the region. As this chapter was written on the heels of the great 2021 season, there is always the chance that the stocks will be decimated over the winter, and we'll be right back where we were in the years when seeing a weakfish was a novelty. I don't like to make fishing predictions because there are too many variables involved. However, I have more than a little confidence that the near future is likely to see good weakfishing because the 2021 run was comprised mainly of 3- to 5-pound fish, as opposed to the much smaller ones that head offshore each fall never to be seen again. Who knows? With a little luck, maybe future high school seniors will have the temptation to skip school for a hot weakfish bite.

Weakfish and bass caught from a Long Island Sound beach in 1981.

CHAPTER 3

BEACH BLACKFISH ON JIGS

Some casts you never forget. This one was May 3rd 1990. The rigging was 20-pound-test monofilament, a flounder hook, a 3-ounce bank sinker, and a sandworm. No serious blackfish angler these days would consider these as a route to a trophy blackfish, but they are easily defensible in the setting of those days. With minor tweaks, they would still catch big *tog* today.

The setting was a Long Island Sound beach at Herod Point on Long Island's North Shore. Winter flounder were still fairly plentiful and large. There was no closed season on blackfish, which saw a tiny fraction of the effort to target them that they see today. Schoolie bass were in good supply, as they still are. There was no such thing as today's braided lines, so monofilament was what was used. As I had done since the 1970s, I was fishing for whatever would bite at the start of a new season, and keeping my options open. The choice of sandworms was an easy one. At that point in the season there were really only four species of fish likely to hit the worms on a Sound beach – blackfish, flounder, stripers, and skates. The odds of catching a skate were actually quite low, so most hits on a sandworm came from a desirable species. Cost was no issue because I dug my own. The bass at that time of year were rarely more than 6 pounds, but the beach flounder were relatively large and averaged around two pounds. Blackfish averaged 5 to 10 pounds and were fairly common.

I fished this application with a #2 Chestertown flounder hook. As far as I knew, the #2 flounder hooks that I bought in bulk and snelled myself were the largest available. I chose them because I didn't want to sacrifice the opportunity to catch the large flounder that were there by using a larger hook more suitable to blackfish and striper fishing. The big flounder hooks were strong enough, in part because the monofilament line had so much stretch that it buffered the force applied to the hook. They would probably straighten with today's no-stretch braid.

Lobsters were also plentiful at that time and I caught plenty snorkeling from the beach. In the process, I learned every piece of structure where a blackfish might hide. One such target is a ledge on the beach-facing side of a huge boulder situated 175 to 220 feet from shore depending on the stage of the tide. The rock is about 15 feet across and just about breaks the surface at high tide.

I arrived mid-afternoon in beautiful spring weather early in the rising tide with the top five feet of the rock exposed. With barely any wind, putting the rig where I wanted with my 10-foot surf rod would be relatively easy. I smirked with satisfaction as the first cast landed inches from the rock, as I knew the carved-out ledge at the base of the rock was directly below. "This won't take long," I thought to myself. Five minutes passed and nothing happened. As strange as this might sound in today's fishery, this was unusual to the point of being unacceptable. The rig should have dropped right in front of the hole beneath the rock, and a blackfish should have hit the worm. Something wasn't right.

I knew the cast was perfect, but was it a little too good? I knew the rock very well. It was flat-sided with nothing sticking out to catch a falling rig. Given the distance the cast came from, it would have entered the water at an angle. I thought it unlikely, but maybe the rig hung on the side of the rock on its way to the bottom. I picked up the rod from the sand spike, gave it a little tug, and watched the angle of the line start increasing. I quickly opened the bail to let the rig fall straight to the bottom. It had indeed been caught on the side of the rock. I engaged the bail, set the rod in the holder, and turned my back as I walked a few yards away. When I turned to look back up at the rod, it was already bouncing.

I snatched the rod quickly from the holder, set the hook hard, but something was wrong. The rod arched over and line ripped from the spool with much more force than should have been possible at this early point of the season. I was totally confused. Having grown up within walking distance from the beach I had already been doing exactly this kind of fishing for more than twenty years. I had caught many large blackfish on this outfit, including some over 10 pounds. This didn't feel like a blackfish. "Striper!" was my next thought as I struggled to pull the fish from the rock, but it was several weeks before the arrival of stripers large enough to exert this kind of power. The hookup made no sense.

Although the boulder was huge, it was a loner with no associated rocks to form crevices for a fish to bury itself in. Despite its size, the rock didn't even produce many lobsters. There was just the ledge that provided shelter from overhead, but not much in terms of a place to break me off if I pulled straight from the beach. As if the fish knew that, it didn't go right back to the rock, but instead went down-current. I knew exactly where it was going. There was a hidden blackfish rock around 125 feet to my left, and I couldn't stop the fish from swimming there.

I followed along as it pulled parallel to the beach. It wasn't taking line as much as it was towing me along. Its progress slowed as it approached the area where the next rock was. This was a good lobster spot because it was a big rock around ten feet in diameter with another rock right next to it. I was finally able to hold my ground without the fish making headway, but realized that was because I was stuck. Because the tide wasn't far from low, and the slope of the beach and bottom isn't very steep there, I immediately walked into the water and headed for where my line pointed while I held the bent 10-ft surf rod above my head. I knew I could walk out pretty far, and hoped I could get enough of an angle on the fish to pull it out. When I reached the limit of my chest waders, I decided my best option was to keep the rod high and pull steadily rather than open the bail and risk the fish swimming between the two submerged rocks, if it hadn't already. As I pulled back expecting the line to break, the solid hang gave way to dead weight. Rather than pump the rod, I just held it high while I backpedaled to the shore, dragging the fish away from the structure as I went.

I had tired the fish significantly before it reached the snag, and it seemed totally spent now. When I made it to shore I worked it in slowly, knowing there weren't any more significant obstructions while worrying that the line might be damaged and would break from any sudden applications of pressure. As the black mass began taking shape in the clear cold water, I began laughing. This blackfish was so big it looked silly. It was so high that it bottomed out around ten feet from the beach. It was much bigger than any I had seen before. Pretty good for the first cast.

It was still alive when I got it to Rocky Point Fishing Stop where it weighed more than 15 pounds. A few days later I heard it had been selected for the cover of the *Long Island Fisherman Magazine*. The next issue indeed had a huge beach-caught blackfish on the cover, but it wasn't mine. Someone caught a 17-pounder from the Sound at Prybil Beach in Glen Cove just in time to bump mine from the cover. To prove I wasn't just lucky to catch a teen-weight beach tog, I pulled a 13-pounder from that second rock on May 1st of the following year. That fish hit at 7:40 p.m., just as I was about to pack it in. Looking back, I'm rather horrified that I kept and ate both of those fish. Various blackfish weight/age charts show the 15-pounder was at least 25 years old. I release fish half that size these days.

While a substitution of braid for monofilament line and a stronger hook could convert the rig I used 30+ years ago to one that would be completely appropriate today, I've gone another route. Fishing for blackfish has soared in popularity in recent years, driven in part by fishing for them with jigs. Correct or not, the fisherman I think of first as a pioneer of blackfish jigging is John Knight, who is associated with Tidal Tail jigs. When I first heard of putting crab on a jig instead of a standard hook and sinker rig, I thought it was some sort of a gimmick. After all, the jig wasn't being used as a lure as is the case in normal jig fishing. It was being used as a bait delivery method. Why not just put the bait on a hook and send it to the bottom with a sinker? There are several advantages to the jig. First, the rig is greatly simplified, and the offering is put on the bottom with the minimum weight possible. Maybe the biggest advantage is that there is a direct line (main line connected to leader) from the angler to the jig. This yields unparalleled sensitivity which is what allows one to distinguish the pecks of interference fish from the movement of a blackfish. Even if the hook is placed above the sinker on a conventional rig, the sinker interferes to some degree with that sensitivity. Finally, when you hook a fish on a jig, there is no dangling sinker to get snagged on the bottom structure.

Blackfish jigging from boats and kayaks will be the subject of the next chapter. The key to the jigging approach is the use of thin braided line, generally not thicker than 15-pound-test. The lightest jig weight that can

A 15-pound blackfish caught from a Long Island Sound beach in 1990.

keep the bait from washing away in the current should be used, and it's best if that jig does not exceed 1.5 ounces. I had already converted to jigs for fishing for blackfish from boat and kayak, but had never seen anyone try it from the beach. I could understand why anglers might be apprehensive. The technique depends on the use of relatively light line, and this would be a problem pulling fish away from structure given the angle from the shore to where the fish is hooked. Recalling that I had caught so many big blackfish from shore on 20-pound-test monofilament, I saw no reason why the use of 20-pound-test braid would be any less effective. Besides, most braided lines break well above their rating. Twenty-pound-test isn't ideal for boat fishing, but you have the advantage there of being able to pull the fish straight up, so 15-pound-test or even 10-pound-test could get the job done in many places. There was only one way to find out if it would work from the beach.

The first thing to do was to figure out where to fish. This was easy where I grew up near the Long Island Sound beaches in Miller Place and Wading River. The beach and bottom slopes are gentle there. At low tide a long tin cast would reach only about eight feet of water, so the largest boulders within casting range are often exposed or create a visible rip with moving water. This made it easy to see and aim casts at the likely blackfish structure. You could literally hit some of the rocks with your casts. This is much harder on the North Fork where the water depth drops off quickly and you can easily hit 25 feet of water in some areas with a good cast, regardless of the stage of the tide. There are not many places where candidate rocks break the surface. While the rock-strewn points are obvious choices for structure, the currents are fast on those, making jig fishing difficult. I wanted to test the jig fishing with slower current. How could I cast to rocks that I couldn't see from the beach? The solution was to use rocks I could see from above on Google Earth.

For my test trip I chose three submerged rocks to try. Using Google Earth Historical Imagery, I went back to October 2017 satellite images taken over clear and calm water. I looked for dark masses that indicated

The Navionics App can be used to help mark and find hidden blackfish structure.

boulders, then used the Google Earth measuring tool to make sure they were within casting distance. I wasn't sure how far I could cast a jig and crab, but figured anything less than 175 feet off the beach was fair game. I moused over the boulders of interest to get the GPS coordinates, then entered those into the Navionics App on my smartphone. Once on the beach, I would position myself well away from the water's edge, but lined up as best I could with a targeted rock marker on the app. When walking toward the water, the app would draw a line in the direction I was moving. By adjusting my path I could put the line over the marker and know exactly where along the beach the boulder of interest was located. That left a little guesswork in knowing how far out the rock was, but within a few casts I could usually find it with my jig.

I geared up with an inexpensive 8.5-ft Tsunami Trophy surf rod with a Penn 4000 reel spooled with 20-pound braid connected to a 3-ft leader of 30-pound-test Fluorocarbon. I brought jigs in the ¾- to 1.5-ounce range, along with some Asian shore crabs and green crabs. The water was glass calm and the tide nearly dead low when I started. It wasn't that I chose these conditions for blackfish, but rather they weren't great for anything else, so at least I didn't feel like I was wasting good fishing time if I didn't catch. I brought my usual North Shore lure bag with me in case something popped up unexpectedly.

"Build the bite." is something we say on the boat when we fish for blackfish. The idea is to give a spot some time, because as the first cut crabs leak some scent in the water, a few fish are likely to show, and they'll attract other fish. For whatever reason, blackfish seem to attract other blackfish. When diving, I saw that some rocks would have none at all, where a nearby rock would have dozens. It's important to not stay too long and beat a dead horse when searching, but don't be in too much of a hurry to move either.

I prepared the first green crab as I would if I was fishing from a boat. Using scissors, I cut the crab in half length-wise and then cut the legs and claws off. I left the shell on. At times when I've fished deep water and strong currents in a boat I've removed the shell to reduce current drag, but I felt it was better to leave it on in this setting for casting distance and to give the larger fish time to get to the bait before all of the little fish had the chance to clean off a piece of crab with no shell.

I was excited to feel bumps on the end of the line on only my second cast, and even more excited to hook the fish. It was indeed a blackfish, but one that turned out to be the smallest of the trip. Within a few more casts I was basically on *lock and load* fishing, with hits coming almost immediately when the jig hit the bottom. As I've learned by observing my baited jig with an underwater camera, these are not individual fish, but swarms of mixed size blackfish along with occasional porgies, sea bass, and other species. The small fish usually attack the bait first, so the key is to wait through all of the little bites until a fish large enough to swim away with the jig grabs the offering. When you feel the jig move steadily, you set the hook as hard as your tackle can handle and then put the pressure on to keep the fish out of the rocks.

I had my 3 fish at 16+ inches limit on the first rock I tried. I never saw the rock, but I felt it with my jig a few times. I interrupted my blackfishing briefly to catch two False Albacore when they popped up in casting range and I switched quickly to a Deadly Dick tin. Both the second and third rocks I tried gave up three keepers each. Most of the keepers were in the 16- to 17-inch range, but my best was a solid 6-pounder. I added 18 short blackfish and one small striper to the trip.

I was shocked at how good the results were, and equally as surprised that I didn't lose any jigs. Subsequent trips showed very few jigs lost as compared to fishing with a hook and sinker rig. This made sense when I thought about it. First off, there's less to snag because there is only a

A quality beach blackfish that hit a jig.

jig instead of a sinker and a hook. Also, the jigs are so light that they don't sink into the structure. Finally, the S&S Skinner Blackfish/Porgy jigs that I use are designed to sit on the bottom with the hook pointing up. This makes them better at hooking fish, but harder to catch on the bottom. I expected to break off fish, but even the six-pounder was handled easily. Again, there was no sinker to get caught in the structure, so once I set the hook, it was just me and the fish and no different than striped bass fishing.

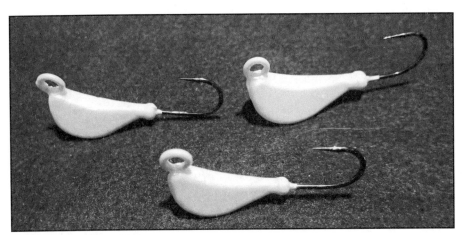

S&S Skinner Blackfish/Porgy jigs.

I started with a 1-ounce jig on the test trip, and moved to a 1.5-ounce when the current picked up. It's best to choose places where the current isn't very strong. Any jig color will probably work, but blackfish are curious so I use bright colors like orange or chartreuse to get their attention. I'm not going to claim credit for starting anything, but after publishing a popular video on that first trip, I began seeing surfcasters carrying blackfish jig rods and small crab buckets with them on North Fork Fall trips. Whatever their motivation was, it made perfect sense. Fall striper and bluefish action is nowhere near as dependable on the eastern Sound beaches as it used to be. By adding a blackfish jig rod along with some crabs, beach anglers could pass the slow times with fun blackfish jigging. Even if you release them all, it's the sort of thing that can keep you busy and on the beach until the next school of albies or something else pops up.

No one with fifty years of beach blackfishing experience will tell you that the fishing for big fish is even close to as good as it was thirty plus years ago. I can tell you that, thanks to the evolution of fishing tackle and techniques, today's fishing is more fun than it used to be if you choose the right gear. I'm not sure we'll ever see another beach fish like the 17-pounder that bumped me off the magazine cover, but there are plenty of 17-inchers to bend the rod and land on the dinner table.

An aggressive fight with a quality beach blackfish.

CHAPTER 4
BLACKFISH JIGGING FROM BOAT AND KAYAK

"Where do I even start?" was my overwhelmed reaction to the sight in front of me as my 16-ft tin boat rounded the boulder-covered shoreline of Rocky Point on Long Island's North Fork for the first time. Looking west, it seemed almost like too much of a good thing. There were rocks everywhere along the shore up to the size of small cottages. It seemed only logical that the rockpiles would extend out beneath the water as well. The chart on my plotter showed some marked rocks, but I understood that most of the rocks were not charted. Finding fish is often easier when you locate the equivalent of an oasis in the desert, such as a rockpile in an otherwise sandy area, but the sight before me showed uninterrupted blackfish structure as far as the eye could see. To complicate matters, I had never fished for blackfish anywhere within 25 miles of my current position.

No matter what I fish for, I'm a big fan of edges, so I selected an area that I knew from my shore-bound albie fishing experience had several hundred yards of clean bottom terminated on a rocky point. I like focusing on edges because they tend to concentrate fish. I could envision blackfish moving inshore as the waters cooled and then moving along the shoreline and setting up when they first encountered appropriate structure. I also knew from albie fishing and studying charts that this was one of the places where you could hit 25 feet of water with a good cast from shore. Even though I was in the boat and could fish anywhere, I had learned through 40+ years of blackfishing from shore, boat, and kayak that October blackfish are often close to the beach in less than 30 feet of water.

After throttling down on the point in 25 feet, I began watching the fishfinder. There were no rocks marked on the chart, but I knew enough to ignore that as my fishfinder lit up with structure big and small. I motored around for a few minutes before dropping the anchor up-current of the highest piece of structure. Even though the main current was moving water into the Sound from east to west, the water under the boat was moving very slowly in the opposite direction. From ten plus years of beach fishing this area, I understood that the current here swung hours before high slack. I also knew that I had about ninety minutes before the current would be running too hard to jig fish.

My jigs were new as in they were still in the development stage with Stanley Gola at S&S bucktails. I had asked him to make me some blackfish jigs with hooks that were strong enough for large blackfish but small enough to catch quality porgies. With that, the S&S Skinner Blackfish/Porgy jig was born. I had Asian shore crabs for bait. These invasive critters infest the local rocky shorelines and are awesome blackfish bait deserving of some ink.

Asian shore crabs are native to the western Pacific Ocean from Russia along the Korean and Chinese coasts to Hong Kong. It is speculated that they were introduced to the United States through trade ships' ballast discharge. They were first observed on the New Jersey coast in 1987, and are now established from Maine to North Carolina. Flip over almost any rock in the lower part of the intertidal zone of Long Island's North Fork, and you'll find these crabs of varying size scattering. Most are around the size of fiddler crabs, but many are significantly larger and approach the size of the small green crabs sold in bait shops. If you have access to a rocky beach in the Northeast, check under some rocks and see what you find.

I had no idea what to expect as I sent my ¾-ounce jig to the bottom with two medium crabs attached. The hits were immediate as soon as I made contact with the bottom. Understanding that the somewhat high frequency little taps were not what I was looking for, I left my jig on the bottom until the bites stopped about ten seconds later, then reeled up an empty jig. The next offering was met with the same little taps for the first few seconds, until I detected the distinct steady feeling of a fish swimming off with the jig. I set hard and the little 6-foot rod barely budged as the fish tried to get back to the structure. After a brief tug of war I had my first legal blackfish on my new waters. My 4-fish limit was filled in about 45 minutes, along with plenty of fun shorts and several sub-legal sea bass. With some new knowledge and fish in the cooler and an accelerating current, it made sense to look for more spots.

As far as I could tell, I was the only boat in sight that was blackfishing. I lived close to this area and understood that this was pretty normal and that the area wasn't fished heavily. There were many rocks charted on my plotter, so I decided that given the almost non-existent fishing pressure I could try any of those rocks and not have to worry much about it being fished out. I chose one that I thought would catch the least current because it was only a few casts off the beach and away from the main points.

Whether you use Navionics, Coastmaster, or some other charts on your plotter, they are crucial to learning to fish a new area. It never ceases to amaze me that I can watch my boat symbol slide over an obstruction mark on my plotter and then simultaneously see the structure sketched on my bottom sonar. We've come a long way since shore ranges and flashers. The chosen rock was right where the chart said it should be, rising about 10 feet off the bottom in slightly less than 30 feet of water. Not being entirely familiar with the current direction on these unfamiliar waters, I missed the rock on my first anchoring attempt. It was easy to make an adjustment and get it right the second time. This would be the last season that I would use a conventional anchor, as the boat hit the water the following season with a Minn Kota trolling motor that could anchor the boat precisely with a button push. We'll address that in Chapter 10. For now, I'd have to tolerate a little bit of swing on the anchor line that comes with using one conventional anchor. It made no difference, as the fish were plentiful and chewing.

As good as the fishing was in the first spot I tried, this was much better with a higher keeper to short ratio. As the current strengthened, I went from a ¾-ounce to a 1-ounce jig to keep the offering from sweeping away. Since I already had a limit on ice, I wasn't measuring fish here, but I released easily two more limits to a little over five pounds. It was an awesome first blackfish trip on the new waters.

Walk into a Northeast tackle shop these days and you're likely to see a large display of jigs used for targeting blackfish. This wasn't the case prior to around 2015, but blackfishing with jigs has since exploded in

A Blackfish that fell to Asian shore crabs on a jig.

popularity. This is very similar to what has occurred with the Summer Flounder (fluke) fishery since around 2010. That was about the time anglers began to open their eyes to the better and more enjoyable catches made while light tackle jigging with bucktails and Berkley Gulp, as opposed to dragging natural bait such as squid and spearing on the bottom. Some charter boats now cater to anglers looking to fish only jigs for tog, and each year more anglers are converting from conventional fishing. The reason is that under many conditions, jigging is not only much more enjoyable, it is also more productive. That said, if you're fishing an area of deep water with strong current, jig fishing will not work well because the lightweight jigs won't hold bottom. We'll address that a bit later.

Jig fishing was discussed in the previous chapter, but let's look at it in detail here from a boat and kayak fishing perspective. The fishing starts with thin and smooth braided line. I use 15-pound-test, but I know successful jig anglers who go down to 10-pound-test. What you choose will depend on the environment you're fishing. If it's bottom rubble that doesn't rise very high off the bottom, you might get away with 10-pound-test. I tend to fish a lot of high boulders that rise more than 10 feet off the bottom. It is nearly impossible to hold fish off this kind of structure because, even if you're able to move the fish off the bottom aggressively in the first seconds of the fight, they don't need to regain that ground against the drag. They need only to swim laterally to rub the line on some part of the high rock. In this situation I want the added buffer of using 15-pound-test.

The use of thin braided line is crucial in order to reduce line drag in the water and allow the use of the lightweight jigs. We routinely fish in water as deep as 40 feet with jigs as light as a half-ounce, though ¾- and 1-ounce jigs are more the norm. I rarely target blackfish with jigs heavier than 1 ½-ounces, although I have caught blackfish in the Fishers Island Race with jig weights up to 3 ounces. I'm fortunate to fish with some pretty skilled blackfish jiggers, and something that's become very clear is the importance of fishing as little weight as possible. If you're fishing ¾-ounce jigs and your line is straight up and down, take the few seconds to switch it out for a half-ounce jig. You want that crab bait to feel as natural as possible when a blackfish picks it up.

I, and everyone else I jig with, use spinning gear for this fishing. Why I use this over conventional or baitcasting gear is one of the most common questions I get. I'll explain, although the answer might get some *buts* and *what-ifs*. When I'm rapid jigging for fluke, I typical use baitcasting gear. I'm right-handed, and like many anglers in the Northeast, I was brought up with right-handed conventional reels. I jig and hold the rod with my right hand. When I feel a fluke hit, my left hand goes above the reel, I set the hook, and my right-hand shifts from the trigger grip of the rod, to the reel handle to crank. It's all very comfortable and natural to me, and most importantly the left hand being above the reel gives me the leverage required for a hard hookset and strong fight if required. I'm often asked in that fishery why I don't use a left-handed reel, and my answer is I wouldn't get as much leverage with my hand under or slightly behind the reel. For what it's worth, everyone I fluke fish with also fishes righthanded baitcasters for that fishery. I fish spinning for blackfish because I feel like I can get cranking with power faster than I can with a baitcaster. My hand is often on the reel handle knob of the left-handed spinning reel as I set the hook, or immediately on the hookup, and I can start cranking right away to keep the fish from structure. I also feel that even a 2000 size spinning reel with a properly designed handle and knob, the Tsunami Evict is an example, has more cranking power than the baitcasters I use for fluke. Finally, the advantage of using a baitcasting reel with a flipping switch for fluke drifting is that you can control the clutch with the thumb bar. This allows one to let out small bits of line to stay near the bottom while drifting. This is not an issue when anchored for blackfish, where you leave the jig on the bottom and don't need to let line out periodically. In this case, there's no advantage to the baitcasting reel over the spinning reel.

The choice of rod for blackfish jigging is crucial, but my description will make more sense after I describe exactly what is happening when your baited jig hits the bottom. After many failed attempts, I used an underwater camera drone that fed live video to my phone to get my jig drops in the camera's field of view so that I could watch exactly what was happening on the bottom. When your jig hits the bottom and you feel bites, it's natural to envision a fish there. The reality with this fishing is that there are probably ten or more fish going after your bait. The first ones there are probably not the larger blackfish that you want to catch, but rather a mix of small blackfish, porgies, bergals, and sea bass. They take turns pecking at the bait until, hopefully, a larger blackfish picks up the bait and swims away with it. Once you've watched it unfold on video,

A variety of small fish swarm a baited jig as a larger blackfish seems curious about the camera.

it translates beautifully to what you feel on the tip of your rod. It's a great demonstration of why you absolutely must wait through the little bites. It may happen that you wait until the hook is clean. Fine. Nothing is accomplished by swinging at the little fish and it just might be the case that the little fish cleaned the hook before a larger blackfish got to the bait. The objective is to distinguish between the small interference fish hits and the pickups of the blackfish. This is where having the right action rod means everything.

Rod action is described with terms like fast, medium fast, or moderate. What this describes is the rod's taper. Fast means that there's a fast transition from the relatively small diameter of the rod near the tip to the larger diameter near the handle. A rod with a soft tip but lots of backbone would be described as fast action. For much of my fishing, including fluke jigging and surfcasting, I prefer moderate action rods that bend in the middle and show a parabolic bend under pressure. This is exactly the wrong rod for blackfish jigging. A proper blackfish jigging rod has a soft sensitive tip that shows every little tap. When a bigger fish picks up the jig, this tip section has a little give. While the soft tip is crucial, the ability to set the hook and move a fish away from structure is equally important. This is where it's important to have stiffness between the handle and first guide nearest the handle. This is what gives you the power to fight the fish. The fast transition from the soft tip to the stiff section near the handle is the very definition of a fast action rod. For me, there's one other requirement. I do not want this rod to be longer than 6 ½-feet. My favorite blackfish jigging rods are a little shorter than this. Some of that is personal preference, but I notice the guys I fish with also use rods in the 6- to 6 ½-foot range for blackfish jigging.

OK, so you have that perfect rod that meets the above requirements and it's matched with a 2000 to 3000 size spinning reel filled with 15-pound-test braid. The only thing left is the leader. I use roughly 4 feet of 30-pound-test Fluorocarbon as a leader. Anything lighter than that will be more prone to fraying on structure. You could probably use 40-pound-test, but I'm finding leader breaks to be rare with 30-pound-test. At the end of your leader is a ¾-ounce jig with a piece of crab attached. How you drop your rig to the bottom and what you do as soon as it's there can make all of the difference.

When you're dropping a light payload from a spinning reel, there might be some resistance as the line comes off the spool. You'll experience an exaggerated example of this on the first drop of a trip because the line and salt have dried and it takes a little pressure to pull line off. Beyond that first drop, you might still feel resistance on subsequent drops. If you do, minimize it with upward sweeps of the rod with the bail open to assist with pulling line off the reel. Do this while watching your line carefully. When you see your line float, you've hit the bottom. Now engage the reel and make very light contact with the jig to feel it, but very importantly, do not apply pressure. You want to feel the fish without them feeling you. If there is significant current, then some tension on the line will be unavoidable while the current pushes on the belly of the line. You should try to minimize the amount of time between when your jig hits the bottom and you engage your reel and make contact because the bites sometimes start on the way down, before the jig ever hits the bottom. You need to be ready in case a nice blackfish is first on the bait.

In the story at the beginning of this chapter, I was fishing with Asian shore crabs. Most blackfishing is done with green crabs, as they are

Michael Skinner putting the pressure on a blackfish while spot-locked over a boulder in 30 feet of water.

reasonably priced and readily available at most tackle shops. Some shops may also sell white crabs, which blackfish sharpies favor when the waters cool. Those crabs also have a good reputation for catching the largest blackfish. In both cases the crabs are cut in half, or even quarters when the crabs are large. Small green crabs can be fished whole on the jig, but it's a good idea to crush the shell or snip off the front of the crab to let some juices out. In either case I cut off the legs and claws with scissors. I hook the crabs through one leg socket and out another. I prefer to leave the shell on to give a little protection from the small fish. If there is substantial current and you're having trouble keeping your baited jig from drifting away, you can try removing the shell to reduce drag.

A word of warning about green crabs – they can burn your fingers! If you store them in the water in a bait cart, then this is not a problem. However, if you leave them out of the water for a few days, their fluids leak down through the crabs, and if you don't rinse them well before use, your fingers could be burning before your trip is even over. I've had this happen and am very careful now, but since I do a lot of blackfishing in the fall, the crab juices still wear off my fingertips to the point that I'm unable to unlock my phone with my fingerprint until I stop handling crabs for a couple of weeks.

While those green crab juices can do a number on your fingers, they also do a great job of attracting blackfish. If I have Asian and green crabs with me, I'll always start a trip with the greens to get the juices and oils into the water. If you've seen the underwater video described earlier, you'll see that actual chum is not necessary, and I would argue that it's counter-productive because it will drift away from your boat drawing fish with it. Even one jig with crab on it is enough to attract fish within a short amount of time.

If you're in an area with blackfish, how do you find those blackfish hotspots? As described earlier in the chapter, there's no shame in fishing rocks marked on your chart plotter. Even if your craft only has a fishfinder, you can install a Navionics App on your smartphone that can give you this information. I have nice plotters on my boat and kayak and still get the app because it has a feature called *relief shading* that really allows the structure to jump out at you. Besides, you can be anywhere with your phone and explore bottom contours with the app for use at another time. The ideal feature to have on your boat or kayak is side-scan sonar. With this I'm able to detect boulders up to 400 feet on either side of my boat and put marks on them for further evaluation. This is how you can quickly find great spots that aren't on the charts and known publicly. Even if you have no electronic charts of any type but only have a fishfinder, you can get a very good hint at nearshore structure by looking for rocky areas on the beach and then cruising over the waters in front of the beach rocks to search for submerged boulders or rockpiles. Some kayaks have no electronics at all. You can still find submerged rocks in some areas because they'll produce a rip with moving water. I don't have side-scan on my kayak, so I'm often moving off course a bit to check out rips and boils on my way to and from fishing spots.

When arriving in an area to fish for blackfish, avoid getting too close to other boats. Although etiquette comes into play here, that's not what I'm referring to. You do not want to arrive on a spot and anchor less than around two hundred feet from a boat that is already there and actively fishing. There's a good chance that the boat that was there before you has sucked in the fish in the surrounding area and has built the bite under their boat. I've watched this happen many times while fishing on Captain John Halkias' charter boat, *Just Fishing*. One of his favorite pieces is an area of rubble and small rocks. He gets there early, and rarely has good action in the first thirty minutes. With time though, the constant crab drops begin to pull in fish from the area, and then he usually does very well. A lot of boats fish the general area around where he fishes, and when they see him catching, they anchor close to him. This never works for the newly arriving boats because John has the bite established under his boat, and they're not going to pull his fish away. The result is the new arrivals catch very little while they watch in frustration as John's clients bail fish. If you're moving into an area with boats, I would stay at least a hundred yards away from the nearest boat. You're better off building your own bite away from everyone.

If you're intent on jig fishing, which I always am, you also need to find places out of the current. In some areas the current isn't a problem. Where I live on eastern Long Island it's a major concern. For me, it often comes down to fishing eddys and places where points break the current. Because these features are dependent on the direction of water flow, I have some places that fish well on outgoing water, but have too much current on incoming. When the tide changes I may need to move to the opposite side of a point to break the current.

Now comes the big question. How long do you give a spot before you move? My strategy depends on how much experience I have with the spot. If I'm scouting new spots, I won't spend more than a half hour on a test drop. If it's a very good proven spot, I'll wait at least twice that long. The half hour on a new spot is to give time to build the bite. As mentioned in the previous chapter, blackfish attract other blackfish. With time you may end up with a lot of them under your boat and near lock and load action. I've also watched on the underwater video how there were only small fish for the first hour, but then larger ones started filtering in. In general, if you have a high degree of confidence with a spot, stay on it and wait it out, unless you have a very convenient nearby option that has similar potential.

As enjoyable and productive as blackfish jigging is, you can't do it everywhere. There are limitations to how much current you can deal with and still hold bottom with a 1 ½-ounce or lighter jig. The Fishers Island Race comes to mind. The Race has relatively deep water and strong currents. It's not uncommon for blackfish anglers to use 16 ounces of lead to stay down. Other than the slack current periods, you can't jig fish in those conditions and a trolling motor won't hold your boat in place. You'll need to anchor and fish conventionally.

Fishing the good old hook and sinker way for blackfish is still fun! It is much more so if you scale your tackle back a bit and fish with 20-pound-test braid, 30-pound-test at most, instead of something like 50+. The thinner braid will allow you to use much less lead. I prefer the use of cannonball sinkers because the round shape has less water resistance and you can get away with less weight as compared to fishing with a standard bank sinker. That round shape will snag less in the structure too. With 20-pound braid and a cannonball sinker, I can usually fish 8 ounces when those around me are using 12 and 16 ounces. Although this style of fishing makes up a small percentage of my blackfish fishing time, I can suggest a simple rig. Tie a surgeons loop knot on the bottom of 40-pound-test leader material for your sinker, a dropper loop around 4 inches above that, and connect a 3/0 to 6/0 Gamakatsu Octopus hook to the dropper loop. Anglers who specialize in deep water and wreck fishing for large blackfish often fish whole crabs on Snafu and other more complicated rigs, but I'll leave the reader to research those if interested.

Fisheries regulations result in the bulk of the blackfish we catch having to be released because either they are too small or a low bag limit has been exceeded. What 30 years ago was primarily a meat fishery, has now transformed into nearly a catch and release fishery. Jig fishing is best for this because it is very rare that a blackfish is hooked deep with a jig, and I've never seen one gut-hooked. Contrast this with the ease in which a fish can inhale a baited hook while the angler's ability to feel the hit is degraded by the weight of the sinker. It's easy to understand why it's so common for a fish caught on a plain hook to be brought to the surface with nothing but a leader coming out of its mouth. Given the slow rate of growth of blackfish, it's a good thing that jigs are pushing plain hooks from the fishery in many settings, because the lower rate of deep hooking should help keep release mortality lower.

In the many settings where blackfish jigging is feasible, it offers the angler a more productive and enjoyable approach that is easier on the many fish that must be released. If you haven't tried it, grab a light spinning outfit and a few jigs and give it a try in areas that don't normally require a lot of weight. Wait through those little bites, set on the steady pulls, and you might find it hard to go back sinkers and hooks.

Captain John Halkias with a quality blackfish caught on a jig.

CHAPTER 5
MY FIRST KAYAK

I bought my first kayak in the late 1990s. It's nothing like my latest plastic craft, and there were two others in between those. Like many other pieces of fishing gear, there's been an evolution. The first one was as basic as they get, but it still sees use a couple of times a year, mostly to get to and from otherwise inaccessible wading spots. The potential for basic transportation for surf fishing factored into the first purchase.

"I can fit an 11-foot surf rod inside the hull." might have been the statement that knocked me off the fence of buying my first kayak. It was part of an email exchange with Manny Moreno. Given that I'd known Manny as strictly a surfcaster, and among the best around, his comment regarding his 16-footer had me viewing a kayak as potentially another tool in a surfcaster's arsenal. The conversation came at a time when some prime surfcasting real estate was frequently inaccessible by 4-wheel drive due to erosion and Piping Plover closures. You couldn't get to these surfcasting hotspots over land, but they could be reached with a short paddle in relative safety as long as you paid attention to the conditions. At this point in my life, I was a hardcore surfcaster with two young children and little time to fish anything but the beach. Fishing out of the kayak wasn't initially much of a consideration. I caught plenty of nice bass from the beach, and my tin boat made more sense for my fluke fishing efforts.

At the time, Wading River Bait and Tackle was in business near my home and they carried the Ocean Kayak brand. This was one of the two brands that Manny suggested considering if I was interested. I would look at them almost every time I was in the shop. "Try mine for the day if you want," the owner, Matt Maccarro, told me one morning. That sounded a lot more fun than continuing on my way to work, so I quickly developed an imaginary ailment, rang work, and then drove off with Matt's yak on top of my Jeep.

Having never sat in or paddled a kayak before, I figured I better play it as safe as possible, so I headed for the freshwater end of the Peconic River. I brought along a rod with a Texas-rigged worm for largemouths. During my grad school days in the Lake Ontario region, I had done quite a bit of largemouth fishing. Two lures covered just about all of that fishing – a black spinnerbait, and a Texas-rigged worm. My first reaction on those first few paddle strokes was amazement at how far the little craft glided across the water when I stopped paddling. This was much different than a canoe.

After about 15 minutes, I forgot about the mechanics of the kayak and began thinking more about fishing. As I worked a shallow shoreline, panfish barely reacted to the kayak passing by. I noticed a log sticking out of the water, paddled up close, and dropped a cast right on top of it. I slid the plastic worm off and saw the line twitch as it sank. As with a hit on a live eel, I dropped my rod tip, watched the line tighten, and set the hook hard. The 3-pound largemouth launched into the air well above my head and landed with a splash that got me wet. I had just received my first thrill of fishing on top of a piece of plastic. The kayak perspective was clearly unique in that I was sitting on the water, eye-level with leaping fish, and able to slip quietly through water inaccessible by other means.

A couple of weeks later, I picked up my new Ocean Kayak Prowler from Matt. I chose olive green for the color so that I would blend into my surroundings and be more difficult to see. The paddle blades were orange, so I painted those green too. I was oblivious to the fact that you want to stand out on the water so that you don't get run over by a boat. The Sit-On-Top craft was 15.5-ft long, 28 inches wide, and weighed 57 pounds. There was no rudder, and we'll get to the significance of that later. I figured the kayak was something that I probably wouldn't use too many times in one season, but I could justify the purchase in the long run. It was just a diving tool for my son and I for the first couple of months, until a late summer day when schools of blues were tearing up the water a few hundred yards off the Long Island Sound beach at the end of my street.

Whether from boat or surf, I don't have much use for 4-pound bluefish. I'm a big fan of large choppers, but under most circumstances, the ones that were pulling me around and nearly bouncing off the side of the kayak were in the nuisance category. So why was I paddling so hard to catch up with the next school? I dismissed the surprisingly fun experience to being a novelty, but it was fun. No mechanical considerations, no noise, fish so close at times that you could almost touch them. Nonetheless, that was it for kayak fishing for the rest of its first year, as there was no way I was going to allow the yak to cut into my surf fishing efforts.

In order for the kayak to be useful for finding dive structure, I outfitted it with a fishfinder and added a mount for my handheld GPS. I knew spots in the Sound that were out of casting range and held quality bass, but I never bothered with them with my boat because I just didn't find targeting stripers from a boat to be all that stimulating. One very bright Full Moon July night of my second season with the yak, I had settled for watching TV because I didn't have any surf options that I wanted to pursue. I thought about how the dead still and bright night would be perfect for the kayak, and how there were probably a few nice bass on

The Ocean Kayak Prowler saw a lot of use as a diving tool.

some 25-foot structure I knew about. I always had live eels in a tank in the garage, and it took very little time to put the yak on top of the Jeep and head to the beach.

In under an hour I was over the spot and saw the fishfinder lit up with fish. The water seemed a little deep for an unweighted eel, so I added a small rubber core sinker ahead of my leader. I cast into the barely moving current and left the bail of my Penn 5500 open to allow the eel to get to the bottom. I had taken just a few cranks when I felt the familiar "bump bump" on the end of the line. I leaned back hard on the medium action 7-footer when the line tightened, and quickly found myself in tow. Only the drag interrupted the silence of the night as I watched the fish break the moonlit surface of the Sound. Hmmm, this was OK. Not so different than what drew me to surfcasting. As I reached my hand down to lip the low 20-pound class striper, I was shocked to see a larger bass following behind. I could never know for sure, but I think it was the same 30-pound class fish that I took on my next cast. I wouldn't be caught watching TV under these conditions again.

When late August came and the fluke were stacked in 40 feet of water off Shinnecock, I couldn't think of a reason why I shouldn't just paddle out to them from the beach at Shinnecock East. I caught some snappers from the shore on the backside of the inlet, was on the fish in less than a 15-minute paddle, and had my 4-fish limit early on my second drift. Catching fluke without a motor while sitting on the ocean was sweet, and each hookup was more satisfying than if I had done it from a boat.

Fall came, and with it, beach damaging storms. The night striper bucktail bite had been red hot on the west side of Moriches Inlet until a storm eroded away enough of the beach to shut down the 4-wheel-drive access, effectively making it inaccessible by land. Cupsogue County Park on the east side of the inlet had good fishing and remained open, but it had become more crowded due to the displacement of the anglers who normally fished the west side. A Nor'easter was almost upon us, and I understood how awesome the fishing on the deserted west jetty would be if I could get there. With that, I began planning for what remains one of my life's most unnerving outings on the water.

The Nor'easter would hit a few days after the New Moon, with low slack water just before 8 p.m. and high slack near 1 a.m. Excessive experience fishing this inlet had taught me that the current there runs in for just over five hours and runs out for nearly seven. I'd be fishing the onset of the storm, with winds forecast in the 25-mph range. My plan was thought out carefully and, even in the worst case, my life should have never been in danger. I would wear a wetsuit so that if the worst should happen, I would be buoyant enough to float and warm enough to withstand the chilly fall water. The straight-line paddle distance was less than a mile, but my chosen route in the shallower back of the inlet to avoid the potential of crossing paths with a boat meant the trip was just over a mile. Even at a leisurely paddling rate, this translated to a 20-minute paddle. I knew this would be anything but a leisurely trip, so it was likely to be closer to 15 minutes because the adrenaline would be flowing and I'd be paddling hard. I carried a safety strobe light in case I somehow became separated from the kayak. All gear would be stowed in the hull, so the only thing above deck would be me and the leashed paddle. Timing would be everything.

I set out from the campgrounds on the east side of the inlet at slack low water, just after dark. I would have preferred to make at least one crossing in the daylight, but I would have nothing to do with outgoing current. With the help of Google Earth, I had carefully mapped out my route on my handheld GPS, which was mounted in front of me on the kayak. The wind was solid from the east-northeast at around 20 mph with gusts to 25 mph. The on and off drizzle reduced the illumination from the Long Island mainland, around a mile and a half away, but it still was not completely dark. It was excellent fishing weather, and I knew I was going to crush the stripers.

With no discernible current, the first trip across was uneventful and full of anticipation. I wore a neoprene surf top over my Farmer John wetsuit, so I was warm and mostly dry. When I reached the other side, I ditched my kayak in the grass, laced up my spiked Korker wading shoes, and retrieved the rest of my gear from inside the hull. This included my rod, bag, belt, and jetty gaff. I was so excited to fish that I nearly sprinted the third of a mile across the barrier island to my favorite casting rocks. As expected, I was the only person on that side of the inlet. I owned the west jetty of Moriches on the onset of an October Nor'easter. Holy crap!

The flood current was already strong enough to bucktail, no doubt helped along by the onshore flow. I snapped on a wine-colored 2.5-ounce homemade bucktail with a 6-inch red pork-rind strip and fired the cast slightly up-current to my right. I let it settle to the bottom before giving it a solid lift and then a crank on the reel to make contact with the jig. I maintained my feel on the jig as it slid down-current, tapping bottom occasionally. I was slightly surprised that I didn't get hit when the jig crossed in front of me. When it reached the point when I'd normally reel the jig back in and try again, I instead allowed it to sweep in closer to the rocks, well down-current of my position. This would not have been possible if other anglers had been there, but the rocks were all mine this night. I was just about to burn the jig back when a solid whack on the rod tip kicked in my hook-setting reflex. The fish put a heavy bend in the rod as it used the current to take line against a tight drag. Several minutes later I descended to my predetermined landing rock and lip-gaffed the 28-pounder. This was just the start.

The next several hours saw intense fishing. I never broke 30 pounds, but I had a lot of fish in the high teens to high 20s. The water was not yet so rough as to make landing them dangerous, and I used my light much more than I would have if there had been other people fishing around me. The hours of great fishing went by fast. Although I never like having to leave a good bite, I wasn't going to deviate even slightly from my plan of departing well before the current turned to outgoing.

I didn't notice it much while I was busy with all of the fish, but it was raining hard now and was very dark. I understood that I would make the trip entirely by GPS, but I failed to anticipate how hard that GPS would be to read in the heavy rain. This wasn't my worst oversight. The paddling trip was not straight jetty to jetty, because there would be no way to get the kayak up and down the rocks. The inlet itself is only 800 feet wide at its narrowest point, but I paddled around a half mile along the back of the east side and then another quarter mile along the back of the west side to have sandy launch and landing points. With the incoming current being pushed by the easterly wind behind it, I was about to embark on a quarter-mile paddle into the force of the current combined with a solid 25 mph wind in my face before I would reach the main inlet, where I would then paddle perpendicular to the current. The chop and almost nonexistent visibility would make it that much harder. This particular kayak cuts current and choppy waves like a knife, but this was a bad situation. I left myself plenty of time to get back to the east side before the current turned to outgoing, but I failed to take into account the time it would take to clear the western backside paddling into wind and current.

When I hopped on the kayak and began paddling, I immediately lost 20 yards of ground before I could build up enough speed to overtake the combined wind and current forces on the bow. For the next ten minutes I paddled with everything I had along the short backside stretch of the jetty. The lack of a rudder caused me to have to occasionally take consecutive strokes on the same side of the kayak to maintain my course, and this broke whatever momentum I had. As dark as it was, I could still make out the pitch-black silhouette of the jetty against the almost black background of the ocean horizon. It showed I was making steady but very slow progress. That rate of progress increased slowly as I approached the jetty's back corner until I crashed through the rip there and emerged in the main inlet current which now ran at a 90-degree angle to my paddling path. I was spent, but thought that should be the worst of it. I would be back at my Jeep soon. There was only one concern left.

I was well aware of an area of breaking whitewater that forms in the back of the east side of the inlet. There was so much white water there on many of the nights I fished that it was visible from the jetty even on a moonless night. What I did not take into account was that I'd be blinded by the wind-driven heavy rain hitting me in the face while crossing the otherwise choppy inlet. Whether I'd intersect this rough patch depended on my path, but I had no clue what that was other than I was paddling east while the current pushed me north. All I could do was paddle and hope I'd miss it. While it took a long time to traverse the first quarter mile along the backside, the next quarter mile was going fast. I was looking forward to the current direction bending east and helping me along, but there was a nagging perception that the water was getting louder.

With no visible land at this point, I had my head-mounted light on and was using it to read my GPS to try to monitor my progress. The primitive unit's backlight was too dim to see in the bad weather. By the time my light caught the whitewater, it was only 30 feet off my bow, and I realized that what I was hearing was the breaking waves in the rough patch and I was seconds from being in the middle of it. *Avoid it or capsize* was all I could think as I made a hard left turning the kayak directly in line with the current as I paddled as hard as I could. Making it to the

Jeep was the last thing on my mind now, as all I wanted to do was beach the yak on the island in the back of the inlet, about a third of a mile north. The combined force of the current and my frantic paddling put me there in about three minutes.

It felt great to stand on land again. Now I could regroup, dry off my GPS, and make a clear plan for the safest route back to the Jeep. I spent the next several minutes wading northeast along the island shallows with the kayak in tow. I kept going until my new route was a half-mile paddle across bay water, well away from the inlet. The current was weaker now than when I started, and the wind and rain were no longer in my face. The paddle from the island to the Jeep was done in about ten minutes.

I had the worst-case scenarios covered on this trip, and although the realization that I could capsize in the whitewater was unnerving, I knew it wouldn't kill me. I would have held onto the kayak and waited until the current pushed me to calmer water. Then I would have righted the craft, climbed back on, and kept paddling. I practiced capsizing and recovering the first day I ever used the kayak. The ease with which this can be done is the reason why all five kayaks that I now own are Sit-on as opposed to Sit-in kayaks. I did own a Sit-In very briefly. It was a tandem kayak for sale on the side of the road. It was in great shape, and for $200 I thought it might be something I could use with family members. The first evening I owned it I took it to the beach with my daughter Katie and we paddled around a bit. It was OK paddling, and for what I paid for it, I thought it was a good purchase until I brought it to the shore for the capsize and recovery test. I intentionally rolled it, and then struggled to bail the water out of it. I'm fully aware there are ways to do it properly, but I had no interest in learning and having to potentially deal with a kayak full of water, so I sold it for $300 the following week.

Even after I bought a more advanced version of the Ocean Kayak Prowler several years later, I continued to use this one for transportation to the frequently inaccessible west side of Moriches, as well as the west side of the Fire Island National Seashore (FINS) breach. To this day, when I need a kayak to sandbar hop for fluke in the South Shore bays, this is the one that gets the nod because it's the lightest kayak I own and paddles better than the Ocean Kayak Prowler Trident that's the subject of the next chapter.

MY FIRST KAYAK

An 11-foot surf rod fits inside the hull, making it an excellent craft to access prime surfcasting not accessible by 4-Wheel Drive or on foot.

CHAPTER 6
KAYAK UPGRADE

It was a sickening feeling. The ocean looked calm, even felt calm, but why was the beach disappearing periodically as I paddled toward the shore from a mile out? This fluke trip in my first kayak was successful, but now it was time to head in and it became clear that the small swell I paddled through in the morning had grown. As this was August, rolling around in the wash should not be much different than any summer swim, but what about my gear? There was plenty of safe storage inside the hull, but the only access was in the bow. That works fine on land, but safely getting close enough to the hatch while on the water would not be trivial. I decided I had to get it done, as my odds of a smooth beach landing were not looking good.

I disconnected my fishfinder and GPS unit so that I could store them, but also because they were blocking my way to the hatch. I positioned my two rods on the deck with the butts facing the bow so that I could reach them from up front. With a maximum width of only 28 inches, I found I could hang a leg over each side and straddle the craft as I shuffled toward the hatch. I needed to reach the center of the rather large hatch to undo its buckle. I was a little worried that shifting my weight almost all of the way forward could lift the stern from the water, but I was able to reach the hatch strap before it came to that. I carefully unsnapped the buckle with one hand, and moved the cover to the side. I realized how ridiculous this must look, sitting almost on the bow of a kayak in the ocean, but it was what needed to be done. I was nervous about the hatch being open because I realized that should I flip, water could flood the inside of the hull. I carefully reached behind me and began retrieving items to put in the hatch. First the fishfinder and handheld GPS, then the two rods and my tackle bag. I was relieved to close the hatch and make it back to my seat. Now I just needed to deal with the surf landing. I took consolation in knowing that some people actually take their kayaks to the beach to ride waves, although they typically don't use 15-footers.

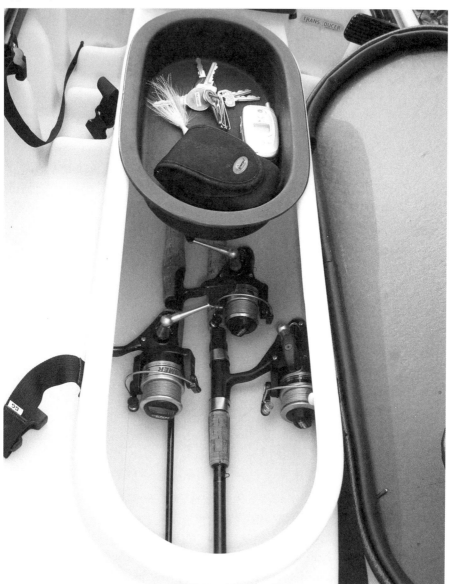

The Ocean Kayak Prowler Trident had a Rod Pod feature that allowed access to the internal storage of the hull from the cockpit.

When I reached the outside of the small breakers, it didn't look too bad. I had driven the beach looking for a launching and landing point that was far enough from any sandbars that would cause waves to build. I observed the waves for a few minutes, chose a lull, then paddled as hard as I could until what was probably a 2-footer grabbed control. I rode it for several seconds and into waist deep water before the bow veered suddenly to my right and I went over. There was a rope tied to the bow exactly for this situation, so I grabbed it and pulled for the beach with the rope in one hand and the paddle in the other. The following wave pushed the yak into me, knocking me down into knee deep water. I held onto the rope to let the wave retreat, then pulled the kayak high and dry. Other than providing somewhat embarrassing entertainment for the beachgoers enjoying the summer weather, the landing was no big deal.

It wasn't long after that trip that I saw an advertisement for Ocean Kayak's next version of my kayak. This was the new Prowler Trident, and it had the features I knew were lacking on my current craft. Very importantly, it had what they called a *rod pod*. This was an elongated hatch in the cockpit that provided access to the inside storage of the hull. From the normal sitting position, it was possible to stow and retrieve 1-piece 7-ft rods from this storage. Now everything of value could be stored safely inside the kayak for surf launching and landings. The new kayak also had a "sonar shield", which was a little compartment ahead of the cockpit made for a Humminbird fishfinder. The compartment had a cover that shaded the unit when in use, but would cover it up when folded down. One of the scuppers was designed specifically for the fishfinder's transducer. This new kayak was very well thought-out. It was around 13 pounds heavier than my current kayak, but some of that was due to the addition of a rudder.

Crossing Moriches Inlet in the middle of the night in a storm had already taught me the value of a rudder, so I was willing to spend the extra 25% required to have that feature on the new kayak. When I bought the first kayak, I thought the rudder price was steep compared to the rest of the craft, so I didn't go for it. I understood the value this time around. Whereas the first kayak was mostly a utility craft, the new one would be a fishing machine. I chose yellow this time, having learned that blending in with the surroundings isn't a great idea when kayaking among boats.

I wrote extensively in my previous books about bucktailing out of this kayak for fluke and stripers. From the ocean, to the bays behind the barrier islands, to the rocky sound shorelines, my Prowler Trident jigged up a lot of fish. It also made an enormous contribution to my beach catches as I learned tube and worm trolling, and quickly found that the stealth of a kayak combined with the deadly tube and worm was an invaluable tool for finding productive surfcasting spots on Long Island Sound.

"Seriously? Bass hit this?" was my reaction to the first time I dragged a tube and worm through the water and watched it corkscrew behind the new Trident a couple of hundred yards off the beach in Long Island Sound. At this point I had lived in Wading River for more than twenty years and was completely familiar with the main boat trolling spots along the Riverhead Town beaches. I didn't fish them myself, but learned where they were simply by being on the water a lot, either diving, shore fishing, or fluking. I didn't pursue these fish because I had no interest in dragging umbrella rigs behind my boat for stripers, as a handful of local anglers had been doing for years. I just didn't see the point, as catching fish on heavy conventional gear using lead line just wasn't very appealing. If I could catch them in my kayak with more civilized tackle, that would be a different story. The challenge was that these fish were in mostly 16 to 25 feet of water, which required some sort of lead to get down to them. The problem was solved when I read an article in *On the Water Magazine* about New England boat anglers trolling tubes on braided line and using various weight egg sinkers to tune in to the desired depth. I found it attractive for the depths I was interested in, as it appeared I would need nothing heavier than a one-ounce egg sinker. When I learned that I could use Gulp worms instead of real ones, I was sold. I had no intention of purchasing and storing live worms, most of which would inevitably be devoured by sea bass and porgies.

T-Man Custom tackle in Connecticut had the trolling tubes at the time, as did many other sources, but what attracted me to their business was their *Quick Change Weighted Keel*, which allowed one to easily change weights without any cutting or retying. I placed an order of several 15-inch tubes, a couple of keels, and two bags of assorted egg sinkers. The egg sinker weights ranged from 1/8-ounce to 1-ounce, which would provide easy fine tuning of weights since the keels had enough room for more than one egg sinker. With the addition of some 6-inch Gulp worms, I was set to go.

A trolling tube tipped with a 6-inch Gulp blood worm is deadly on big bass in the shallows. Weight can be added ahead of the tube for deeper trolling.

Ideally, you buy these things, let your line out over a spot you think has fish, engage the reel, and then the rod would bend over with a fish within a few seconds. Things rarely work out that way, but amazingly, that's how it played out for me. The 26-inch bass was no trophy, but it was proof enough that the technique would work over the spots I was interested in. The added benefit was that this was a summer afternoon that had me catching a bass in a bathing suit while on the kayak.

The rigging is straightforward, but I make an important modification to the weight keel. It comes with decent quality swivels on both ends, but I replace them with Tactical Angler clips and add high quality ball bearing swivels to those. The ball bearing swivels promote tube spinning while reducing line twist. The front ball bearing swivel is attached with a Palomar knot to the braided main line and the rear to a roughly 36-inch Fluorocarbon leader with the trolling tube on the end. I use 50-pound-test for both the braid and the leader. Thirty-pound-test would work for these, but the 50 is more abrasion-resistant around the rocks. Many anglers will tip the tubes with real sandworms, but I do just fine with Gulp worms, which hold up much better to the porgies and sea bass. If you get a few raps from one of these interference fish, the Gulp has a good chance of not being torn, which means you will probably still have a whole worm on when you encounter the bass. The real worms tear easily.

Trolling speed is roughly 2 mph. Depending on current speed, you add a little going with the current, and subtract a little going into it. I find myself mostly going between 1.8 and 2.5 mph. This is a very comfortable trolling speed for a kayak, as it requires only leisurely pedaling or paddling. A pedal kayak and its ability to provide nearly hands-free operation is much easier than using a paddle kayak, but that's what I had in the beginning and I did fine. It's hard to beat doing this kind of trolling with an electric trolling motor, and I've been doing exactly that in recent years with my 16-foot tin boat, and the electric kayak described in Chapter 11.

Medium power tackle is good for this. I usually use spinning tackle because that's what I learned with, as I found it easier to let line out in spurts with the rod in the rodholder while paddling. Now that I either pedal or use the trolling motor, light conventional gear works just as well, if not better, because you can thumb the line as it's going out.

My spinning rod choice is a relatively inexpensive Tsunami Classic 7' H. It's deceptively underrated at 12- to 25-pound-test line, but I've whipped 100-pound-plus Florida sharks with it. Although I normally pair this rod with a 4000 series reel, I go up to a 5000 for this kind of trolling so that I can have a little extra cranking power in the structure.

Even with the upgraded swivels, you may still encounter line twist, as the tube is constantly corkscrewing through the water. I would suggest setting aside a dedicated spool of line or reel that's used only for tube trolling so that you don't twist line you'll want to cast with. I have no need to troll in water deeper than 25 feet, so I never need to go heavier than a 1-ounce egg sinker on the keel. If you want to troll deeper, you can buy larger keels that will handle 2 to 10 ounces of weight. If you're too heavy, you'll know it in a hurry as you'll be hitting bottom and picking up bottom growth and/or snagging bottom. If you're seeing bottom bumps, lighten up a bit on the weight. With some experience in a given area, you'll know exactly how much weight to use for a particular stage of the tide. If you're trolling in 10 feet or less of water, you can leave off the weighted keel altogether and attach the braid directly to the ball bearing barrel swivel of the leader.

The extraordinary value of tube and worm trolling is that it is way more productive than it should be, and the word "magic" comes to mind when I think of it. Its power is that big bass inexplicably pound this offering regardless of time of day. On smaller bay and sound waters, this makes the technique an ideal tool for searching for hidden bass hotspots within surfcasting distance from shore. It was the weightless shallow trolling that led to a couple of shore-fishing honey holes, and one truly exceptional spot in particular.

A big bass that hit a tube mid-afternoon off a Long Island Sound beach.

CHAPTER 7

FINDING A HONEY HOLE

"I think I found a gold mine," was my answer to my wife's "How was fishing?" question when I returned home from a late summer kayak trolling trip. I had almost literally connected dots, and halfway between them located a pile of big stripers. I knew enough about the area and the behavior of the stripers there to know that this was not going to be a one-off catch. I had located a honey hole.

"Fish swim." It's a statement I've heard from people trying to encourage others not to chase fishing reports. The meaning is that fish are always on the move, so just because you know where a bite was yesterday, they're probably gone today. In many cases, it's true. I can tell you that for at least the last 30 years, when I've heard or read the "Fish swim" statement, I quietly thought to myself "No they don't." Yes, of course they swim, but there are some small spots that hold stripers year after year, decade after decade. I know of only four, and one of those is out of shore casting range. To be clear, I'm not talking about a typical good fishing spot, like maybe the tip of an inlet jetty or stretches of the Cape Cod Canal. Those are good places to fish because of features that bring high quality bait in a disoriented state where stripers can feed easily. If there's no bait, there are likely to be few if any fish. I'm talking about spots in Long Island Sound where stripers stage. I know spots in that body of water because I've lived within walking distance of it most of my life. I suspect there are other bodies of water with hard structure that have similar hotspots. By *hard structure*, I mean rock features that are not impacted by storms. They're the same as they were a hundred years ago and they'll be the same a hundred years from now. A sandbar near an ocean beach is what I'd call *soft structure*. Such structure comes and goes with storms.

I'm writing this in the middle of a 90-degree mid-summer day with full confidence that if I dove those four spots at the instance I'm typing these words, I would see stripers in all of them. One of the spots looks pretty good from standing on the beach. One looks like everything else in the area. You would walk right by the best of them because there is so much better-looking structure nearby. I know, because I walked past it for years without realizing that by expending the effort to make very long casts, I could have been picking big fish on pencil poppers. If you're a long-time follower of my YouTube channel, then you've seen me pull numerous 20- to 30-pound plus stripers from it in the daylight. This is the full story of how I found it.

The frustrating thing about knowing the location of a magic spot is the thought that there are probably several more like it within a few miles to either side along the shore. The problem is that finding them can be like finding the proverbial needle in a haystack. Another frustrating thing is that you need to protect them. If someone is fishing nearby, you have to leave it alone and not give it away because such spots are typically small and hold a limited number of fish. This is where it helps to have alternates, so if for some reason you're worried about exposing a spot, you can simply go to another one. You can certainly never have too many. With this in mind, I'm always trying to find new spots where stripers congregate.

It almost always starts with satellite imagery. It has never put me right on a honey hole, but in this case it got me close enough. This whole area looked awesome from beach level, with plenty of boulders breaking the water. From the sky I could see that there was a slight drop-off going west to east. I know now that at low tide the water depth is six feet going to eight or nine feet, so this was nothing drastic, but that two- or three-foot difference was exactly the sort of drop I had in my best spot. I'll call that *spot #1* for clarity in this chapter, and it was only two miles away and had given up 20- to 40-pound-plus bass for years.

This spot of interest, I'll call it *spot #2*, was in the back of my mind for years, but I could only be in one place at a time and I was busy with spot #1. It was only on the rare occurrence that I was concerned about blowing my main spot that I would do a little fishing around spot #2. I caught fish there, better ones than in most of the surrounding waters, but only teens at best. Any time I spent there on the productive dusk through dawn tide window was time taken from a nearly sure thing with big fish, so my efforts there were very limited. This all changed when I learned the kayak tube and worm fishery.

At first, tube trolling was just for the fun of catching big bass in the kayak. Kayak fishing is similar to surf fishing in terms of aesthetics and challenges in so many ways. The first year or two of kayak trolling was done with weighted tubes in the 15- to 25-foot range, and well off the beach. One of my most major shore fishing breakthroughs came when I had the idea of trolling weightless within casting distance of shore. As mentioned in the previous chapter, tube and worm trolling is such an effective way to catch quality stripers during the day that it seems to defy striper fishing logic. This was the key. I could now leverage the effectiveness of daytime tube trolling to allow me to research new spots during hours when I wouldn't normally be shore fishing. Suddenly I could explore without cutting into my productive shore fishing windows.

Spot #2 was at the top my list. My first attempt was on a late summer afternoon. I paddled east on my first approach and started on the shallow side of the slight drop and out of casting range, as my track was somewhat constrained by rocks sticking out of the water. Before I even made it to the drop off, the rod was yanked back so hard that it was a struggle to get it out of the rod holder. I was only a little disappointed to see it was a big blue. I understood from deeper trolling areas that big blues were often in the same general areas as the bass, although they weren't necessarily mixed. I repeated the approach with the same results. I started my third pass closer to the subtle drop-off, and this time made it across unscathed by bluefish.

Because I had cleared some rocks that were in the way, I could now angle in toward the beach. I did this while watching the fishfinder carefully and straightened my track when I saw the water depth decrease quickly from 9 feet to 6 feet. This was a contour line that ran parallel to the beach, and a huge feature of interest for me. If you've ever seen lines of trap buoys set in Long Island Sound, these are almost always set along the contour lines because the fish run along them. I had barely straightened on the contour line when I was hit hard again, but this time the line that was departing my reel angled down instead of toward the surface. The teen bass was just the start. It's an exaggeration, but the saying "I couldn't keep a line in the water" came to mind for the next two hours as I fought almost constantly with 12- to 25-pound bass, and only a rare blue.

One of the problems with searching for fish from the shore is that it's very difficult to cover ground while casting for maximum distance. It's easy to wade along in waist-deep water, but it's another story if you need to be well up to your chest where you need to find a perch to stand on in order to fish comfortably and effectively. It was now obvious that my previous shore-bound efforts on spot #2 suffered from this. I was clearly on a good concentration of fish with the kayak, but I was also out of normal shore-casting range. I had it now though, as I chose some shore rocks as markers that I could use to know where I needed to be along the beach to hit these fish. When I got home, I went back on Google Earth to look for candidate perches. When I went to the beach the next time, I did it with a wetsuit to see exactly what was available to me in terms of rocks that I could stand on within deep-wading range. I found one that worked well, and it was not something that I ever would have found if I wasn't highly motivated by the kayak fishing success. The fish on the back cover of *Striper Pursuit* was caught from that rock, as were many others through the next season. The kayak had proven its worth as a beach fishing search tool, and I wanted more.

A problem inherent to daylight plugging an exceptional spot that no one else knows about is that it takes some effort to keep it that way. It's hard not to be constantly looking over your shoulder. One morning while fishing spot #2, I saw another caster headed in my direction. I recognized him from a distance, but was pretty sure he didn't know who I was. I had a long running reputation as a productive surfcaster at this point in my life, so it would have been potentially quite bad if he recognized me. I got away to the east, likely with him having no idea who I was. After all, he was just fishing, and I was being paranoid and trying to protect something. If you're reading this Al, try a hundred yards east. After putting a safe distance between the two of us, but not so much that I couldn't keep an eye on him, I made a few plug casts over a spot with some boulder rips and caught a 12-pounder. I looked at it on Google

Earth when I got home, and saw a couple of sizeable boulders on the edge of shallower water. A few days later when low tide was in the afternoon, I did some snorkeling there and was excited to see three bass that were probably in the 10- to 13-pound range. I could usually expect to see no bass when diving random spots on the Sound. I had done a lot of this over the years while lobster diving, so seeing three bass together was significant. The next time the tide was low enough in the evening to reach the spot with an eel, I caught three bass there, topping out at about 13 pounds. I thought it was probably a coincidence that I saw three diving and then caught three eeling. It sure looked good, but a couple of subsequent shore attempts yielded nothing. It remained a point of interest that we'll call spot #3, and it was 0.3 miles from spot #2. It was time to work this over with the tube and worm. Because my launch spot was west of spot #2, I'd be trolling across that first, and then eastward to #3.

Moving at the 2-mph tube and worm trolling speed, it would take about ten minutes to troll from spot #2 to spot #3. They were close enough that I decided to troll from one to the other. The first pass produced nothing. I reeled my rig in to make sure the worm hadn't been cut by a sea bass or porgy, and then reset the troll to go back from #3 to #2. Now I'd be trolling with the current, which is always my preferred direction. That said, I've caught plenty of bass trolling into the current.

My main focus was on the two spots, so I made sure I led #3 by enough distance to get my line far enough behind the kayak when I passed over it. I moved my track in slightly, not seeing the point in repeating the previous path. The pass over #3 yielded nothing, so I paddled toward #2 with no expectations of anything happening until I got there, as the water and shoreline between the two was free of boulders and looked quite boring. Halfway to spot #2, I was startled to see my rod yanked back to a screeching drag. The roughly twenty-pound bass ran toward the shore and briefly hung me in some hidden structure before I pulled it out. This was a pretty nice fish for 3:30 in the afternoon on a late summer day in eight feet of water. After releasing the fish, I paddled back east far enough to reset the line and run over that spot again. I decided to follow the track line exactly, rather than move in a little to where the fish hung me. At about the same point along the beach, the rod pulled back so hard that the kayak turned with the screaming drag. I was soon hung again, and within several seconds of pulling the fish out, hung yet again on a second hidden rock. This fish would top 40 pounds, and had no business being where it was on a summer afternoon, unless I had just found a special spot. That both fish hung me on the same spot was very interesting. These fish weren't just passing through, they were familiar with the structure. A third repetition of the trolling pass produced another 20-pounder, that also ran into rocks that even on satellite imagery were barely noticeable.

I lost all interest in catching more fish at this point, focused instead on doing what was necessary to hit this precise spot from shore. I landed and released the third fish very close to the rock it hung me on, so it was easy to paddle over and mark it on my plotter. I then paddled into the beach and got out of the kayak in shallow water while lining up the mark so that it was straight out from my position. The tide was up a couple of hours at this point and a little deep to wade, so I used the kayak to find a semi-flat rock that would make a good perch for shore-wade casting. While positioned over that rock, I took a pair of shore ranges. One was a pointed rock at the waterline lined up with one at the base of the bluff. That would give me the correct east/west coordinate. For distance from

The 40-pounder that hit in 7-feet of water on a September afternoon within casting range of the beach.

shore, I lined up a rock in the water with a very large rock a quarter-mile away on the shoreline. I would satisfy those two range requirements many times in the coming years to locate my new casting perch. From there, a roughly 250-ft cast would put me on the fish. This was doable with a pencil popper, although disappointingly, not with much else. I couldn't come anywhere near it with a live or rigged eel.

I had to wait only a few days for an early morning low tide to test the beach approach. I started on spot #2, sort of as a control, and was disappointed to do nothing there. If I didn't catch on the new spot, it wouldn't necessarily mean I was off or that it wasn't a good spot. As all anglers know, sometimes fish just won't eat. Slightly past low tide, and only twenty minutes after sunrise, I made my first cast onto the new spot. It yielded nothing, but I felt as though I might have been slightly left of where I wanted to be. I corrected on the next cast, firing it slightly to the right and up-current of what little current there was. The video shows that it was eight seconds before the initial blowup, followed several seconds later by a firm hookup and strong run. As with the kayak fish, the cow hung me momentarily in the rocks, and weed hung off both the line and plug as I worked the 33-pounder into the shallows. This would become my best plugging spot until I eventually abandoned it years later after my move to Greenport. Because the spot was between Greenport and my day job, I hit it a few times before and after work on prime tides. Although I continued to pull fish from it, I knew in the back of my mind that I would never bother to drive west once I retired, which was coming soon. I never did a "last trip" there, but just stopped going as I focused on finding spots closer to my new home. It's not that I'm lazy, but I don't like to lose time driving.

Although I have beautiful video of finding the spot by catching those fish in the kayak, I never published it on YouTube, knowing that there were too many landmarks in the background to put it out there for tens of thousands of people to watch. Knowing that I was done with the spot, I finally released the video on my *Salt Strong* striper course. I'm not sure if anyone ever nailed it down from that, as I was more concerned with applying the same search methods thirty miles east.

The first of many large bass caught over a number of years from a surfcasting spot discovered while tube trolling the beach.

CHAPTER 8
THE PEDAL KAYAK

While my second kayak was a step up from the first, the next one was a leap. I realized it on the maiden voyage of my 2019 Hobie Outback pedal kayak when I lost my drift while targeting fluke in Shelter Island Sound. Seeing "0.0 mph" on my plotter told me something needed to be done. Not being able to cover ground on scattered fish is a poor scenario for any fishery. With my other kayaks I would have had to paddle slowly with my rod in a rodholder, but then I couldn't put that all-important jigging action on the rig. I had watched enough underwater video to know that motion in the strike zone was the key to attracting and enticing fluke. For the first time in a kayak, I could propel the craft with my hands free.

The "0.0" drift was no longer an issue. I put the pedal drive in reverse and pumped the pedals slowly while watching the speed on the plotter, settling in at the ideal fluke drifting speed of around 1 mph. Taps on the jig followed by an arched over rod told me I had it right. By pedaling in reverse, I was able to keep my line in front of me. Combined with the higher seat position of the Hobie as compared to my previous kayaks, this made for a very comfortable jigging position.

I realized quickly that I now had perfect drift control. Wind against current was no problem because I could just pedal into the wind with sufficient force to keep my line near vertical as I jigged. Instead of using a drift sock when it was windy, I could just pedal into the wind to slow the drift. This worked much better than a drift sock because, as with using the pedal drive to compensate for wind against current, I could vary the force I was exerting into the wind so that I could keep my line close to vertical. This enabled me to use lighter weight jigs, which is always a positive when jig fishing.

It was on this first trip that I experienced another advantage that was on par with the new found drift control - I now had more range. The current that runs between Greenport and Shelter Island is strong. The bite I had early in the tide was rather slow, although I caught a few short fluke and a nice weakfish. As the current picked up steam, that bite died. I told myself at the beginning of the trip that the goal for the afternoon was to learn the new craft, and any catching would be secondary. I was very comfortable with the kayak at this point, and was beginning to think more about the fishing. If I was on my boat, my next move would have been to a spot around a mile and a half away, up along Shelter Island. Because I was now off East Marion, this meant having to cross through the strongest current. I decided to try for the spot and test the kayak and my ability to propel it.

Pedaling on an angle to the current, I was able to move at 2.5 mph. Around half-way there I noticed that I wasn't tired, just a little bored, so I had a snack while I pedaled. Roughly 35 minutes later I arrived at the new spot. While I could have probably made the trip in one of my paddle kayaks in a similar amount of time, I would have been much more tired. Everything I had read about pedal vs. paddle kayaks in relation to leg muscles being more powerful than arm muscles was clearly true in my case. I felt fine, which was important because my first drift in 45 feet of water showed a speed of 1.2 mph, and I would be pedaling into that before each subsequent drift.

The first drift produced nothing, so I moved in a little closer to an edge at around 40 feet. A feature of fishing the waters between Greenport and Shelter Island is near constant boat waves. While I was never overly concerned with flipping in my other kayaks, this one was noticeably more stable, which wasn't surprising given that it was shorter and wider. My jigging began getting interrupted by what felt like a fluke toying with the rig. I just kept it moving and finally felt steady weight. I set the hook hard and the rod doubled over on what was clearly the best fish of the trip. The excitement turned to frustration as I promptly lost it. Ninety seconds later I set the hook again on the feeling of weight, and the rod barely budged. There was a lot of resistance on the first several cranks, but then mostly weight and classic fluke headshakes. I strained my eyes through the turbidity but saw nothing until the 8-pound-plus fish with my pink teaser in its mouth took form about a foot beneath the surface. I anticipated it being a good one, but its size still caught me a bit off guard. I kept it moving all of the way to the net. As the first of what would be many fine Hobie catches thrashed in the cockpit, I declared mission accomplished. After one more uneventful drift, I headed for the launch point.

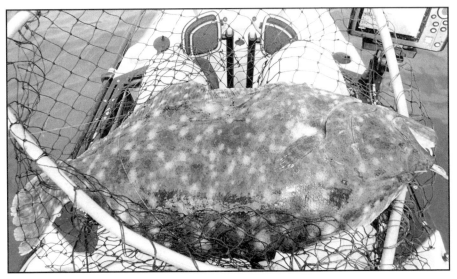

The fish that made the first trip in the Hobie a big success.

Back at the beach, it was time to deal with the one downside of this versus my other kayaks – increased weight. Although this Kayak was almost 3 feet shorter than my other two, it was 6 inches wider and weighed 85 pounds stripped. That was about 15 pounds more than the Trident, and nearly 30 pounds more than my original Prowler. The shorter length however provided me with an option that wouldn't work with the 15-plus-footers. Now I could use a bed extender on my short-bed pickup, and forgo having to somehow get the yak on top of the vehicle. The bed extender was a $50 model from Harbor Freight. I duct-taped a pool noodle to the top of it to protect the bottom of the kayak. At its lowest setting the extender's crossbar was just slightly higher than the bed of the truck, which was perfect because gravity could help keep the kayak in the bed. I needed only to lift the stern onto the padded crossbar of the bed extender, disconnect the dolly that I used to move the yak from the water's edge, then lift the bow to about waist-level and push it in. Bungie cords secured the kayak sides to the truck bed railing system, and I was good to go. This was faster and easier than roofing either of my lighter weight but longer kayaks.

The Hobie became my go-to kayak for all of my kayak-based fishing, except for applications that required surf launchings and landings. The Trident remained my preferred craft for those trips because of the ability to store my rods, tackle, and electronics inside the hull. My first season with the Hobie saw plenty of use for summer bay fluking behind the ocean barrier islands, as well as the Long Island Sound fall fishery that included blackfish, albies, and stripers. As much as I enjoyed fishing from it that first season, I couldn't have anticipated how important a craft it was about to become.

A bed extender can provide a convenient kayak transport option.

CHAPTER 9
ADAPTING TO A NEW FISHERY

I could see the radar gun pointed at me from at least a half a mile away. The white car with lights on top angled almost perpendicular to the road stood out like a sore thumb. Under all other circumstances my reaction would have been to tap the brakes, but just this one time I momentarily went for the gas before thinking better of it and slowing down. I regret that decision to this day, and wish I had made the Brookhaven Lab police officer pull me over for speeding on what was my last trip out the gate after 28 years of working there. Getting pulled over for speeding out of The Lab on my retirement day would have been a classic exit, but "Do it!" lost out to my urgency to just get home and continue packing my fishing gear. In three days I'd be headed to my new winter home on Pine Island in southwest Florida, and a whole new fishery to focus on.

The 0.08-acre tiny plot of land on the dead-end of a canal in St. James City had been purchased 12 years earlier and served as a retirement dream. Almost a year earlier we had signed the papers to have a manufactured home placed on it. That home was finally all complete with electricity and running water, and my wife and I were on our way. The one thing it lacked was a dock, as that had been tied up in unreasonable permitting complications. With very little shore access on the island and no desire on my part to get a boat until I had a dock, I would be a kayak fisherman for my first winter in Florida. As the move happened in mid-January, this was more like half a winter. In retrospect, being almost totally limited to kayak fishing was one of the best things that could have happened to me.

Up North, a kayak was a nice thing to have because of its ability to be launched almost anywhere that you could park near the water. It was also very aesthetically pleasing to fish from, much like surfcasting. In Florida, I see a kayak as, with the exception of range, a shallow water fishing platform that is superior to a boat. Almost all of my redfish are caught in water that's less than two feet deep. Many of my snook catches are in less than three feet of water. In a few instances I've targeted sharks in a spot I call *the abyss*, because it's so much deeper than the surrounding waters. The deepest water there is six feet. There are of course channels with plenty of water to carry boats of all sizes to and from the Gulf of Mexico, but with the exception of technical poling skiffs, most of those boats can't get at some of the best fishing.

For the first winter it was going to be me and the Hobie. This forced me to find access points scattered on and off the island. If I had a boat docked in the backyard, I would likely have limited myself to the waters in reasonable range of the dock. Distance range would not have been the only constraint, as there would have been the issue of depth range. While experienced shallow water anglers seem to have no trouble running their boats at 40 mph in less than two feet of water, I can tell you that takes some getting used to when you've fished your entire life in waters where three feet was considered very shallow, and hitting bottom was unacceptable and likely expensive. Being "limited" to the kayak actually made so much more water available to me because I could launch it in a hole in the mangroves 30 miles from home if I wanted and never had to worry about going too shallow. The ability to go shallow in comfort was a critical part of my first trip into the new fishery.

"This is about as clueless as I've ever felt," was what came out of my mouth the first time I aimed the Hobie out into Pine Island Sound and began pedaling. There were ten small mangrove islands of maybe an acre or two each within two miles of the general direction I was heading. I chose to fish the area for the simple reason that there was a kayak launch nearby. The pre-trip online research showed the water was shallow all around, with most places reading one to two feet deep on the charts, and an occasional five-foot spot mixed in. Google Earth wasn't much more helpful than the charts, as I could see it was mostly very shallow with deeper "potholes" scattered around. What neither source of information could tell me, and what I considered most important, was the current

The fully geared Hobie Outback resting on a Southwest Florida island.

profile. I considered that the small islands were located almost halfway across the sound, and beyond them were the barrier islands of North Captiva and Cayo Costa. Those two were separated by Captiva Pass, an inlet in my language that was sure to channel lots of water between the Gulf and the Sound. This led me to believe there should be at least some current near the islands. It was time to think like the Northern striper angler that I was. Structure, current, bottom contour, and bait – these were universals in good fishing.

Good structure was a given, since all of the islands were lined by mangroves whose root structures dip into the water and provide a habitat for baitfish and the gamefish that feed on them. I noted a standard 20-something-foot center console boat on plane and passing between two of the islands, so I concluded that there must be some sort of a channel there. I also noticed a relatively narrow gap between two of the islands, so it made sense that the islands deflected current and that the gap should have moving water. I headed for the tip of an island that was a mile and a half away and nearly straight out. I'd start near its southern point and fish the quarter-mile stretch to its northern point. This would give me a shot at channel water on both ends. As I approached the island, I noted a half-dozen white pelicans sitting on the water around 100 yards off the shoreline that I was intending to fish. In surveying everything else in sight, these were the only birds. I took their presence as a sign that there was bait in the area.

I was downright excited when I reached my starting point at the tip of the island, as it was clearly carved out by current to a depth of four feet. This was relatively deep given that most of the surrounding waters were less than two feet deep. I turned parallel to the shore and began making periodic pumps of the pedals to make progress along the shoreline. I was pedaling into a slight breeze that was more of an influence than the opposing incoming current that I was floating on. I had made two backwater trips prior to this one, and had earned a little confidence in two lures – a spook-like Rebel Jumpin Minnow, and a 5-inch Gulp Jerk Shad on a 1/16th-ounce 3/0 swimbait hook. I started with the spook, aiming for underneath the mangroves where I just assumed there would be snook given the deeper moving water. Ten hitless minutes and a hundred yards of shoreline later, I concluded I was wrong.

As I worked that shoreline, I noted an occasional mullet leaping in an area that was roughly mid-way across the stretch that I planned to fish, but at least 100 yards away. I had done enough research to know that, although these mullet were too large to be baitfish for my intended targets, redfish were often found with them. I was interested enough in their presence to stop casting and pedal to them directly. As the water transitioned quickly to less than two feet deep, I spooked something that was too large to be a mullet. I stopped pedaling immediately and traded the spook plug for the jerk bait, casting it as far as I could toward the shore, but only making it about halfway there. I began a slow retrieve with frequent twitches as soon as it landed in the foot-deep water. Most of the way back to the kayak I set the hook on a tap, but but didn't feel anything good on the end of the line until I caught up with the fish swimming at me. "Oh my goodness it's a Red! Holy Smokes!" I said out loud at the sight of the small redfish off my bow. I understood completely that the 20-incher was just a little guy, but it was evidence that maybe my Northern approach to finding Southern fish might just work.

I pounded that 200-yard stretch of the little island for the next couple of hours. With the kayak always in reverse while casting, I backpedaled on fish after fish in an attempt to avoid spooking them by being pulled onto the spot. It worked, as I landed 11 reds and 3 large speckled trout before a guide boat anchored up-current of me and started flinging live baitfish into the water as chum. He was a respectful distance away, but there was no question that my hot bite shut down around 20 minutes after he anchored, which was around the same time the hooting and hollering started on his boat. It was time to explore a bit, so I started pedaling and didn't stop until I was a few hundred yards around the corner of the island, and out of the sight and sound of the guide boat. Mangrove overhangs shaded a 10-foot wide slice of water along the shore from the late-afternoon sun, providing what looked like an ideal place to catch a snook and complete an inshore slam. I never got the snook, but I caught three much larger redfish in the 30-inch class, along with two large trout.

My total take for my first clueless venture into Pine Island Sound was 14 redfish and 5 trout. The success was entirely due to applying what I had learned fishing for stripers in the Northeast. I looked for structure, current, and bait, and found fish willing to feed. The major adjustment in catching these fish was doing it all in less than two feet of water, and the Hobie made it easy.

Access is just one of the kayak advantages in shallow water fishing, the other is stealth. Whether pedaling, paddling, or pushing, a kayak is dead quiet as long as the angler is careful not to bang things around. This allows you to be immersed in the environment without the fish you're targeting being impacted by the presence of your craft, until you hook a fish. This is where it becomes extremely challenging to fish a paddle

John Sweeney with a nice Florida redfish.

kayak effectively. Every decent fish you hook is going to drag the kayak into the area where the fish was hooked, or worse, into the mangroves. When fishing the Hobie I often backpedal on fish to keep the kayak from being dragged onto the spot.

The Hobie is phenomenal for moving slowly and quietly across the shallows. When you fully extend the pedals, the fins lie flat against the hull, allowing the craft to glide in just inches of water. While it requires around 14 inches of water to make full pumps of the foot pedals, you can take short pumps to propel the craft slowly in less than a foot of water. It's what I was doing when I pulled one of my largest redfish in water less than a foot deep.

The conditions were as challenging as could be. The unfiltered sun was already a couple of hours above the horizon and the surface of the very clear water was an absolute sheet of glass as I approached the shallow flat and felt my fins beginning to bottom out. I began taking shorter pumps with one leg extended so that I could keep moving to where I'd turn parallel to the mangrove shoreline.

Understanding that I would be covering water with good potential, I started casting on the way in. The 5-inch Gulp Jerk Shad on a 1/16-ounce swimbait hook was one of two lures that I relied on heavily since coming to Florida. It was perfect for fishing in very shallow water, and could be made weedless if necessary. I was still perpendicular to the shore when I felt a tap followed by steady contact. It's as exciting a feeling as an explosion on a topwater lure, because unlike in that case, you have no clue what has just grabbed your lure. I set hard and line immediately came off the reel as a redfish exploded on top. It was a medium fish of about 25 inches, and I soon had it at the yak and released it.

I resumed my slow approach at the shoreline until I was about a cast and a half off. I then turned into the gentle current and began taking periodic short pumps on the pedals. One short pump every several seconds was plenty to maintain forward motion so that I could work this stretch that had produced well in the previous weeks. There was no need to cast all of the way to the mangroves, as the redfish here were usually a little ways out, such as the one I just caught.

I was making progress along the rather straight shoreline when a sizeable red spooked close to my bow. I took consolation in knowing that I didn't spook it until I was almost on top of it. Given how shallow the water was, it was unlikely I could spook anything here and not know. A nice thing about the jerk shad lure is that it touches down pretty lightly, almost like a small baitfish. As my lure landed on a cast, I saw a disturbance under the line, maybe a third of the way in. I was being careful to keep my rod tip high to keep as much line as possible out of the water because I had seen reds spook from the line before. This fish hadn't swam away though, just moved enough to make its presence known. With a slow but erratic twitching retrieve that kept the jerkshad darting, I worked the lure over where I had seen movement. This time the movement was simultaneous with pressure on the rod tip as the fish took the lure and swam on an angle in my direction. I reeled quickly, setting the hook along the way for a couple of seconds until the fish turned and boiled on top with a bulge that told me I had just hooked the largest red of my two months in Florida. The fish cut in front of the kayak and swam for open water. Its heading was a gift, as I was being pulled away from potential mangrove snags and clear of the grounds the fish were on. The rolls on the surface reminded me of a striper, but this fish had more stamina. After a give-and-take battle that lasted a couple of minutes, the fish barely found enough room to fit in the net. I was careless lifting it into the kayak and broke the net handle in the process.

The Hobie turned out to be the perfect craft to learn the Florida fishery. Because there were many launch point options spread out geographically, it gave me the opportunity to fish places that were not in reasonable

The stealth features of the Hobie Outback make it excellent for skittish shallow water redfish.

reach by boat from my new home. As I write this with an old Maverick flats skiff on a lift in my backyard, I still opt for kayak fishing more than I do boat fishing. With time, as I learn to navigate the shallows with the boat and discover spots that are new to me, that may change. However, the winter river tarpon that are an hour away by car and the Everglades grouper that are two hours away will always be the domain of a kayak, but probably not the Hobie. After all, why do all of that pedaling when you can just push a button and slide quietly across the water under battery power?

A trophy snook that hit a topwater plug on a cold Florida morning. Backpedaling the Hobie kept it out of the mangroves.

CHAPTER 10
GAME CHANGER

Halfway through my second winter in Florida, a tractor trailer pulled up to my home and dropped off my new fishing tool – a 12-foot Old Town Sportsman Autopilot kayak powered by its accompanying 45-pound thrust Minn Kota trolling motor. The term *game changer* is used too frequently in our society, but when applied to fishing with an electric trolling motor, the term is accurate. Even before cutting the shrink wrap off the new kayak, I understood its capabilities, as I had learned these two years earlier when I added a trolling motor to my 16-foot aluminum boat on Long Island. Drifting for fluke and anchoring for anything would never be the same. We'll get back to the electric kayak in the next chapter.

Success in fluke fishing is highly dependent upon having a good drift. Ideally you want to be drifting in the same direction as the current, in the speed range of about 0.5- to 1.5-mph. Because the wind exerts a lot of influence, the drift is rarely ideal. The worst case happens when the wind blows against the current, and the two cancel each other out. In that case you can end up not covering any ground while your offering scopes out under the boat as if you were anchored. While a drift control sock can sometimes improve drift conditions by counteracting the wind component of the drift, it can only help so much. You can use your main engine to backtroll and control a drift, but I find it downright annoying to continuously shift the motor in and out of gear in an attempt to maintain a proper fluke drift speed with the current. At first, I envisioned the trolling motor as a way to deal with the worst-case scenario of wind against current. I thought that its application in fluke drifting would be as a tool of last resort, and I actually didn't use it much through my first two Peconic Bay fluke trips of 2019. Then came the Saturday morning of a stiff west breeze blowing against an incoming current from the east.

The trolling motor providing a fluke drift on a windless day.

An interesting thing about Peconic Bay, as with many other waters, is that you can use local knowledge to choose the direction of current. Although the main current in this area runs east to west on a rising tide, there is some meandering of the waters between the North Fork and Shelter Island. Equally important is that there are eddies where the water runs in the opposite direction of the main current. One of these is closer to the Shelter Island side at Greenlawns. Another is behind town near Claudio's restaurant, a well-known fishing landmark on the edge of the bay. While these examples are specific to this area, eddies exist in many areas of current flow and irregular shorelines. No matter where you fish flowing water, they are good to know about.

On any weekend day in May or June, the eastern Peconics are likely to have a hundred plus boats fishing for fluke. This particular morning was no exception as I could see a large fleet behind town, with the smart ones there no doubt taking advantage of the eddy to put the wind and the water flow in the same direction instead of in opposition. While the Greenlawns were on the other side of a point on Shelter Island and therefore out of my line of sight, I could only assume that there were several dozen boats there as well. Another well-known fluke stretch, and the one closest to my launch ramp, is the old oyster factory area in East Marion. Despite this having at least as much potential as the other two spots, there were no boats there at all. The reason was obvious as the wind was directly against the current resulting in almost no drift movement but a lot of line scope in the 40-ft depths. This seemed like the perfect place for me to fish, as I could use the trolling motor to set the drift I wanted and have the whole area and its fish to myself. This would be rather unheard of on a weekend in May.

My friend John Sweeney installed the trolling motor on my boat with whatever help I could give him. This was no small job, as I counted 13 hours of effort to do the mount and the wiring. I was fortunate that I could fit the two dedicated group 27 batteries inside the console. Battery placement can be a huge consideration with a trolling motor and the distribution of the extra battery weight can be an issue on smaller boats like mine. The installation included a cable connecting the 80-pound-thrust Minn Kota with my Humminbird Helix fishfinder/plotter. Because these two companies are affiliated, the plotter and trolling motor communicate with each other.

I'm normally good about reading things like manuals and instructions before using a new piece of gear, but the simplicity of the trolling motor micro-remote preempted any such efforts. The buttons consisted of on/off, left/right arrows, +/- speed, spot lock, and autopilot. No instructions were necessary for what I wanted on this trip. I was fully aware more complicated functions were available, including the ability to store tracks and repeat them when desired. This would be ideal for running contour lines, but all I wanted this day was a good drift.

This being my third season on these waters, I had marks on my plotter of where I had caught fish previously. I ran a little up-current of these, shut down the outboard, and deployed the trolling motor. Prior to turning it on I observed the drift direction and speed on the plotter. The current was indeed winning the battle with the wind, but not by much. My drift was close to the correct direction, but the speed was averaging only about 0.2 mph. I dropped a line to the bottom out of curiosity, and as expected it scoped out well ahead of the boat in the direction of current flow. I turned on the trolling motor, pointed it in the direction the current was running, then increased the power until my line was nearly vertical and slightly behind me as if I had the ideal scenario of a light breeze with the current. Because of the usual variability of the wind strength and direction, it was taking slight course adjustments every ten seconds or so to stay on the course I wanted. To save myself this effort and distraction, I pushed the autopilot button on the remote. This immediately drew a purple line on my plotter showing me the track that the autopilot would work to maintain. It wasn't quite what I wanted, so I adjusted it with the arrows on the remote, setting the purple track line to pass through marks where I had caught fish before. My course was now fully automatic and perfect. All that was left was the drift speed. Although I could use cruise control on the plotter for this, I preferred to tweak the speed manually with the '+' and '-' buttons on the micro-remote. Cruise control would set a constant speed and adjust the motor's power accordingly. I was more interested in the boat's speed in relation to the current, rather than just the Course Over Ground (COG) speed.

Based on where my trolling motor was pointing on my first autopilot drift, I thought it was malfunctioning. Then I looked at the green line on my plotter showing the boat's actual course, and it was almost perfectly in line with the purple line that showed what I asked autopilot to do. Although the direction that the trolling motor head was pointing wasn't where I'd be pointing it if I was steering manually, it was in fact doing exactly what I asked it to. The little computer inside the trolling motor head continuously adjusted for the complex and variable interactions between the wind and the current, and held me on the exact course I wanted without me having to do anything but tweak the speed occasionally if desired. This freed me up to focus on the fishing.

Under most conditions, I'd be periodically letting out more line to stay in the near bottom strike zone, or maybe adjusting bucktail weights. With the trolling motor giving me a perfect drift, I could stay down with a 2-ounce jig in 40 feet of water and easily give it plenty of bouncing action to attract nearby fish. All of this in an area that was apparently considered unfishable by boats that were at the mercy of the wind and the current. The first drift produced a couple of shorts, so I offset the next drift into slightly deeper water. I was just outside of one of my marks when my jigging was interrupted by that unmistakable feeling of weight. I paused for a fraction of a second to confirm the steady pressure and then set hard. There's no better feeling in fluke fishing than when you yank the rod skyward but it stays where it was with a lot of shaking on the other end. As soon as the 6-pounder landed in the net, I hit the spot lock button on the remote to hold the boat in place while I unhooked and bled the fish. Maintaining position in a situation like this was just one of the many valuable uses of GPS anchoring, where the trolling motor will continuously adjust power and direction in order to hold the craft in place. With the fish bleeding out and my line ready to go back into the water, I could continue my "drift" from where I left off. I caught another short on that drift, but decided to cut it a little short and run over the spot where I had just caught the good one.

It was child's play to stop at the top of the drift and adjust the purple line on the plotter to instruct the autopilot to repeat the previous successful course. I made it only slightly past where I caught the 6-pounder when everything repeated and I put a slightly larger fish in the net. Fishing had been slow recently, so this was relatively excellent fishing that I had all to myself despite it being a weekend and less than a mile from the main town launching ramp. I could actually see my truck from the end of the drift. Those were the biggest fish of the trip, but I added two additional keepers to reach my 4-fish limit. The catch would not have been possible under those conditions without some means of power drifting. The trolling motor made it effortless, as it would on many subsequent trips. Whereas I had originally seen the motor as a last resort option to fight bad drift conditions, it soon saw use on most trips because I became

There are trolling motor models available for big boats. The Minn Kota on this 32-footer is compensating for a wind against current situation while fluke fishing.

spoiled by the ability to easily have perfect drift control. As big a game changer as the trolling motor is for drift fishing, it is even more so for anchoring for blackfish.

With all due respect to blackfish, they can be annoying. Anyone who has targeted these fish with any regularity has likely experienced times when one part of a boat produces much better than another. Yards matter when fishing for blackfish, and a small move of fifteen feet can make a big difference. Conventional anchoring is time-consuming and often leaves you a little bit off of where you want to be, especially when only one anchor is used. Even if you do position the boat perfectly with conventional anchoring, your position is subject to wind and current force and direction. When they change, as they do frequently, so does your boat's position. GPS anchoring eliminates all of that and allows convenient position adjustments necessary to fish atop the most productive parts of a piece of structure.

With conventional anchoring, moves lateral to the current require pulling the anchor and resetting. This eats up valuable fishing time and is often not precise. With a trolling motor, small adjustments are made with a couple of button pushes, and most have a "jog" mode where you can make small moves in five-foot increments in any direction. I can say from experience that I'm more likely to leave an unproductive spot altogether and try another because I know I can anchor easily on other spots without losing time. Trolling motors used to be feasible only on smaller boats, but that has changed. Two of the boats I fish on regularly are 32-footers with twin engines, and the 36-volt Minn Kota motor anchors them just fine in reasonable current. I've only seen the batteries depleted one time, and that was in a 25-knot wind and substantial current pushing in the same direction. A typical full-day trip of anchoring for blackfish rarely runs the batteries lower than half of a full charge. What would it be like to have all of these electric motor features on a kayak? I was about to find out.

The trolling motor's Spot Lock feature is holding the boat over structure and a load of blackfish.

CHAPTER 11
ELECTRIFIED

Understanding what a trolling motor offered, I was excited to be unwrapping my new electric kayak. Over the course of 20 years, this would be my fourth kayak. I had progressed from a plain paddle yak, to one with a rudder, to a pedal Hobie, to finally this one. I had seen makeshift implementations of kayaks fitted with electric trolling motors, but this was the first time I had seen a kayak made specifically for a trolling motor. Because Old Town and Minn Kota are under the same parent company, it was apparently easy for them to work together to develop this new craft. I knew it was well thought-out when I lowered the 24-pound motor into the obvious receptacle and it clicked into place without me having to read any instructions.

My main concerns were alleviated well before delivery. As with the Hobie, most of this craft's use would be in the Florida shallows. How shallow could it run with the motor deployed? It turns out to be about 14 inches, but keep in mind that's with a forgiving bottom where you're unlikely to sustain damage if you run aground. How would I pull the motor out of the water in a hurry when I was about to bottom out? You simply pull the handle on a cord and it tilts the motor out of the water while killing the power. The motor will not power up without being locked in the down position. The motor is redeployed easily by pulling back on the same cord handle.

What about the battery weight and lifetime? This was no place to be cheap. I had no desire to deal with a 62-pound lead-acid battery for kayak fishing, especially when its power would degrade as it discharged. The $700 solution was a 25-pound 100 Ah Lithium-ion battery. These maintain nearly the same voltage until they are around 90% discharged. How long and far could I run the kayak before a 100Ah Lithium-ion battery died? After a year of heavy use including some near sunrise to sunset efforts, I still don't know because I've been unable to kill the battery. From my experience, Old Town understates the battery life. They say that the battery will last 2 hours at full power. At best the kayak's speed is 4 mph at full power, so this translates to 8 miles. I run my motor at 95% power, and several days before writing this chapter I measured a full day trip at covering 10.3 miles, but that was just running spot to spot and did not include actual fishing. On top of that I was spot-locked for almost 4 hours in a moderate breeze. I've also put in long days in the Florida Everglades in strong currents and have been unable to fully deplete the battery.

Sight fishing is popular in many shallow water fisheries. While kayaks are awesome skinny water crafts because of their stealth and shallow draft, most are not easy to stand on to achieve the height necessary to spot fish at a distance. I can stand on my Hobie, but not confidently, and I don't find it easy to transition between sitting and standing. If you're young and athletic, then maybe you would have no trouble standing up from the seated position, fishing while standing, and then returning to the sitting position in a Hobie Outback. I'm not comfortable doing it. Worse yet, once you stand up in a pedal or paddle craft, you've lost your main means of propulsion and direction control. Sure, you can pole a flat effectively, but you can't travel faster than poling speed while staying vertical. Increased stability, a higher seat position, and remote control of the electric motor make this all comfortably possible with the Old Town.

My Hobie Outback and Old Town Autopilot 120 hulls both weigh 85 pounds stripped, but their dimensions are slightly different. The Hobie is 12 feet 9 inches long and 34 inches wide. The Old Town is 12 feet long and 37 inches wide. Shorter and wider translates to more stable. Equally as important for the Old Town being a great standing kayak is that the seat is higher. I find it easy to stand up and sit back down in the Old Town. That extra stability comes at a price in that the Old Town is a barge compared to the sleeker Hobie. I sometimes paddle the Old Town to get through water that's less than a foot deep, but it takes a lot more effort compared to my other kayaks. Of course, this is offset by the fact that the kayak is propelled by the trolling motor most of the time. The ability to run at 3.5 to 4 mph with no expenditure of energy translates to increased range in my case, and I exploited that extra range and other advantages of the motor kayak on a chilly January trip.

The fully-geared Old Town Sportsman Autopilot 120 on a Florida flat.

With only two winters of Florida shallow water fishing under my belt, I understand that there is plenty I don't know about fishing for redfish and snook. One thing I do know is that you can't catch them in areas where there is no water because the tide is so low. It's what I faced as an astronomically low tide combined with a stiff northeast breeze pushed the water out of Pine Island Sound and left my targeted redfish spot with less than six inches of water, and some totally exposed mud/grass bottom. The astronomically low tides are referred to as "negative" tides in my Southern fishery. It's possible that some use that terminology up North as well, but I had not heard the term before. When you look at a tide chart, you'll see two numbers associated with a high or low tide. One is the time that the tide is predicted to occur. The other is the predicted height of the water in relation to mean low water (MLW), which is the height of the water on an average low tide. For example, if you see a listing for high tide of 5.0, this means the predicted height of that high tide is 5.0 feet above an average low tide. If you see a low tide listed for -0.7 feet, this means that the low is predicted to be 0.7 feet below the height of an average low tide. That would be considered a negative tide. In addition, wind has a profound effect on the movement and depth of water in shallow bodies of water. A stiff wind that pushes water out can easily blow away an extra foot of water. If you subtract that foot of water along with almost an extra foot from an astronomically low tide, you can easily have a low tide near two feet below normal. In a shallow water fishery where many of the fish are caught in less than two feet of water, a negative tide combined with such a wind can empty a good fishing flat. That was the scenario that I had on this winter morning.

My plan took it all into account as I motored down a channel toward the middle of Pine Island Sound toward a collection of exposed pilings that had once supported a commercial fishing ice house that had burned decades earlier. The barnacle encrusted pilings situated on the edge of a 6-ft deep channel had proven to be an excellent sheepshead spot for me on a previous trip. I had never ventured the 3.1 miles from shore in my Hobie, but didn't hesitate in the electric yak. My plan was to spend some time fishing the "deeper" water for sheepshead, but then target redfish, snook, and trout as the rising tide filled in the areas on top of grass flats and along the mangrove shorelines of several nearby islands.

Sheepshead are related to porgies, and to me they look like a fancy version of the porgies we catch in the Northeast. There are some differences though. Although porgies will hit small baitfish and are often caught on diamond jigs and other artificials up North, sheepshead eat primarily crustaceans such as crabs, barnacles, and shrimp. Sheepshead grow larger than porgies and fight harder, similar to blackfish. They're a much sought-after fish in Florida waters during the winter, and are a lot of fun to catch, in addition to being excellent table fare.

Most of what I've read about sheepshead fishing involves using a very small baited hook weighted down by either some split shot or a small egg sinker. In the same way that I prefer to jig for blackfish and porgies up North, I'd much rather target sheepshead with baited jigs. One advantage of this approach is casting accuracy. Sheepshead are very much like blackfish in that they are usually very close to structure. I find casting underneath a dock or next to a piling to be a lot easier and more accurate with a baited jig as opposed to a sinker with a trailing length of line leading to a baited hook. As with blackfishing, this also reduces the chance of losing fish in structure, because once a fish is hooked, there's no hanging weight to get caught on something. In my targeted collection of pilings in 6 feet of water washed by a gentle current, a 1/8-ounce jig with a hook of an appropriate size for sheepshead makes the perfect delivery vehicle for a piece of crab or shrimp. With so little weight and no external sinker, it's a very natural presentation method for the often wary and terminal tackle shy sheepshead. My outfit consisted of a 7-foot medium action spinning rod spooled with 20-pound-test braid connected through a small barrel swivel to a 3-foot leader of 20-pound-test Fluorocarbon.

When I arrived at the structure, I hit the anchor button on my handheld remote to engage the spot lock feature on the trolling motor. I stabilized around 25 feet from the pilings, but then disengaged momentarily so that I could drift back a few feet to line myself up with a clear path to cast between the rows of pilings. With only pilings sticking out of the water and no actual dock for my jig to land on, this made for very easy cast placement.

Shrimp are undoubtedly the most heavily used bait for sheepshead fishing, but this is only because they are so readily available and reasonably priced at the local bait shops. My experience, limited as it is, has shown that crabs are far superior to shrimp for catching sizeable sheepshead. I learned this on my first-ever sheepshead trip when I anchored near a dock in the pass that separates Sanibel Island and Captiva Island. I spent an hour and forty minutes fishing with shrimp there for many small fish but only one keeper that was just a little longer than the 12-inch limit. When I switched to the few mud crabs I had brought along, I quickly boated my eight fish bag limit with most of the fish ranging between 16 and 18 inches. With that trip etched into my memory, my bait supply consisted of about 15 small mud crabs that I had gathered from under rocks and oysters on nearby shorelines. These crabs were between the size of the Asian shore crabs and the small green crabs used in the Northeast for blackfish.

The first crab out of the bucket was about the size of a quarter. I hooked it through the leg sockets, pinched the front with pliers to get the juices flowing, and pitched it into the pilings. Within five seconds the rod tip was tapped sharply followed by the feeling of the jig being carried away. I set the hook hard and immediately felt the rub of the closest piling, but I managed to pull it out as the leader squeaked against the wood. The 18-incher was deserving of the net. It took a little over an hour to land my 8-fish limit, which was perfect timing as I estimated that in the twenty minutes that it would take to get back to the redfish grounds, the tide would have risen to the point that there should be enough water on the flats.

Spot-locked near the structure and catching Florida Sheepshead.

I cruised toward the redfish grounds on the electric motor for around ten minutes until the water became too skinny to keep it deployed. A simple pull of the cord popped it up and out of the way as I reached for the paddle that would carry me the rest of the way to where I hoped there would be redfish nearly in the middle of the 500-yard-wide passageway between two islands. As opposed to the 3-ft deep mud bottom channel I traveled out on, this passageway was less than a foot deep with a carpet of beautiful green turtle grass. This was perfect for redfish to feed on as they searched for crabs and shrimp in the flow of the incoming current that was pushing me from behind. In such shallow water they could search the flat in relative safety from dolphins that often patrolled the deeper water. This also set up the perfect scenario for one of the high points of flats fishing – tailing redfish. This occurs when they angle their body down to root out food in the grass and their iconic spotted tails break the water's surface. If that sight doesn't raise your pulse, you need to find a new passion.

I didn't see tailing reds during the first couple minutes of paddling, but I did spook a fish that left a 'V'-shaped wake that could have been a red. When I was getting close to where I had found them on a recent trip, I decided to stand and pole my way with the current. This would slow me down, but give a much better view of what was nearby. As I stood up, I was shocked by the sight of a redfish ten feet directly in front of the bow. There was nothing I could do but watch it spook off across the shallows. I wished I had stopped a hundred feet earlier, but at least I had the right idea about going to this part of the flat.

I poled a little farther, then traded the paddle for my rod rigged with a New Penny colored 5-inch Gulp Jerk Shad on a 1/16-ounce swimbait hook. I would let the current carry me slowly across the flat while I blind cast and scanned for fish. After a few minutes, a slight momentary dimple in the water caught my eye around fifty feet away. Through my polarized glasses I spotted the chunky redfish underneath. With minimal movement I flicked the offering ahead of the fish and worked it slowly on a twitching retrieve, hopefully into its line of sight. Instead of the fish moving toward the lure, it spooked slightly, but only went a short distance instead of heading off the flat like the fish I almost ran over. I made a guess as to where it settled down, and threw well behind it while I continued to visually scan for other fish. Around thirty feet from the kayak a boil appeared simultaneously with a thump on the line, followed by steady pressure. I swung back hard to an explosion of copper on the surface followed by a short run that towed the kayak. Typical of a redfish, it didn't want to give up as it kept pulling the kayak in less than a foot of water until I got a lip gripper on it after a fun two-minute battle. The chunky red shining in the sun was as beautiful as they come.

I spent another thirty minutes looking for more redfish and saw a couple, but couldn't get any to eat. That was fine, as now there was enough water in a spot where I wanted to try for snook. This was a 200-yard-wide passage between two islands and it was narrow enough to generate decent current. The depth ranged from 2 to 5 feet deep, depending on whether you were over a pothole or high spot. Of particular interest was that there was easily 2 feet of water against the mangrove shoreline that was in the lee of the light breeze and faced southwest into the sun. Given that this was relatively cool weather, the sun beating on glassy water would give that shoreline the extra warmth that could help attract snook. Current, structure, temperature in relation to surrounding waters – these were all things I had learned to take into consideration to find snook.

I stayed with the jerk shad on a swimbait hook because it catches everything and was a better choice for snook than a topwater lure would be in cool waters. The current speed was about 1 mph and the right thing to do was to travel the shoreline against the current while *beating the bushes*. This was ideal for the electric kayak because I could set a slow constant speed and direction with the motor and then use the foot pedals to control the rudder. This gave me perfect directional control while keeping both hands free. Ten percent motor power was slow enough for me to cast at all of the little mangrove pockets, but fast enough to cover the 300-yard stretch of shoreline that bordered the passage. I made it about a third of that when a cast placed within a foot of the shore was grabbed about 30 feet out. "Something good!" I declared as I buried the hook on the fish that swam at me while jumping. I reeled feverishly to get whatever line it would give me knowing full well a snook of that size would come to its senses and head for the mangroves. That it did, but the drag stopped it before it could hang me in the roots. For the next two minutes jumps interrupted runs and dives that left me convinced that this fish was going to find its way off the hook. I was most worried about the leader.

When I'm targeting snook, I fish 40-pound-test Fluorocarbon leader. They don't have teeth, but their mouths are rough and the gill plates sharp. Because I was also targeting redfish, I was using 30-pound-test leader because that's about as heavy as I want to go with the more leader-shy

A big tarpon that hit while the kayak was spot-locked on a Florida river.

Stormy wind against current on Shinnecock Bay was no problem as the trolling motor provided a perfect drift, and lots of Summer Flounder.

redfish. When I felt the fish was sufficiently tired and far enough away from the mangroves, I loosened the drag a bit to protect the leader. As I eased the fish to the kayak, the frayed leader was clearly visible, so I went for the landing net rather than the trickier lip gripper or an attempt at thumbing it. It was obvious that one sharp headshake would part the line. I was relieved to see the fish safely in the net, and not at all surprised that a leader replacement was required. The 32-incher was a damn good catch in the cool weather, but added to the previously caught quality redfish, and a limit of sheepshead, this trip was a banner one, and not yet finished. By the time I headed back to the launch point I landed two smaller snook, a medium red, and a jack crevalle. Wanting a speckled trout for an inshore slam, I stopped on a grass flat a few hundred yards from my truck and caught three. Aside from the sheepshead, all of the fish were caught on Gulp or a soft plastic on the swimbait hook.

The trip was a superb demonstration of the capabilities of the kayak. I didn't hesitate to travel 3+ miles to the first spot because the electric motor allowed for comfortable range. I spot-locked on the sheepshead, poled and sight cast to the redfish while standing, then had perfect hands-free track control while motoring into current for the snook. This combination of a kayak and integrated trolling motor was nothing short of an awesome fishing machine.

CHAPTER 12
EPIC BATTLE

Every serious angler has fish battles that stand out. The 5 ½-hour battle with a giant mako shark that I wrote about in *Season on the Edge* was one of mine. What I'll describe here eclipsed it, and will remain etched in my memory for as long as I live. Although the setting is Florida, it was many years before I began wintering there. It was however a factor in my desire to make Florida my winter home.

I felt a rush of adrenaline when I saw the first road sign for the Overseas Highway. I knew I was now only about 120 miles from my next fishing spot – Key West. My brother, Brian, was stationed in the Coast Guard there, so I had a free place to crash for what would have otherwise been a cost-prohibitive dream of a fishing trip. This trip was well-researched and downright cheap. The Southwest Airlines flight was reasonable, but the real deal was that a 7-ft rod tube counted only as one of my two free checked bags. It held four 1-piece spinning rods. The large suitcase was limited to 50 pounds, and I used every ounce of that, weighing it frequently while packing. Its contents included not only the reels, line, and terminal tackle, but also everything I would need to carry a rented kayak on top of the Toyota Corolla rental car that I was cruising down the chain of islands in. Two foam blocks, a bathmat, and four straps would do the job.

This was all necessary so that I could rent a kayak for a full week, thus allowing me to fish as early or late as I wished without having to worry about rental shop opening and closing hours, as I would for a daily rental. After much research, I found Big Pine Kayak Adventures, roughly 30 miles east of Key West. There were many kayak rental facilities closer to Key West, but none that would rent me a fishable sit-on-top kayak for a week at a reasonable price, which was $150. My plan was to fish the flats during the day, then shore fish channels at night for tarpon. The kayak would give me good access to the flats. I had suitable bonefish gear, but was told by a tackle shop that I stopped at on the way down that it was unlikely I would see any. That would be fine, as the big barracuda on the flats could provide more than enough entertainment. The main event was to be the nighttime tarpon fishing, as this was mid-April, and the yearly migration of big tarpon had commenced.

The rental car and rental kayak on the Overseas Highway in the Florida Keys.

My initial plan involved the bridge areas of several channels separating various Lower Keys, but those plans changed when I met my brother on the Key West base and got a look at Fleming Key Cut. The current in the 100-yard-wide channel reminded me of Moriches Inlet, but it was what I saw when I looked at the top of the bridge that quickened my pulse – street lights. Of the 42 bridges that connect the little islands that make up the Florida Keys, only a handful have lights. You don't need them to have good tarpon fishing, but they help immensely by attracting bait. I had no intention of fishing from the bridge itself, as the banks were well-suited for fishing. This was an ideal setup where I could park my car within yards of most of my fishing and, as it would turn out, have the place to myself.

This was striped bass inlet fishing, except for the substitution of a 7-ft rod for my usual 11-ft jetty stick. Two Long Island surfcasters had given me nearly identical advice on how to catch tarpon in the channels at night. One was John Paduano, the other person's name has left my memory, but a key piece of advice that he gave me was to use 100-pound-test leader material. In retrospect, I should have taken that advice sooner. Both anglers told me to use big swim shads. Paduano speculated that the shads did a better job than the bucktail and porkrind combos that we both used in the inlets for stripers because the tarpon seemed to like the vibration of the pulsating shad tail. When a good credible angler gives me advice on a fishery I'm not familiar with, I take it.

My tarpon rod for this trip was a fairly low end 7-ft Penn Legion rated for 15- to 30-pound line. The reel was a Penn Slammer 560 filled with 50-pound-test braid. The terminal end had about a 4-foot leader of 80-pound leader material connected to the braid through a small high-quality barrel swivel. The leader was tied direct to the swim shad.

I arrived on the base to fish just after sunset on the first night, Monday. The beginning of the ebb was barely a trickle, so I spent the first twenty minutes or so of my time there surveying the shoreline bordering the channel to identify rock perches for the night's fishing. I was reassured to see the lights on the bridge already on and bright enough that I knew I would have plenty of light to walk safely on the beachball-sized irregular rocks that lined the edge of the channel. These were not like the rocks I was used to on Northeast shorelines, as they were much more porous. I thought maybe they were limestone, or even coral, but I didn't care much beyond the fact that they were "grippy," and sneakers would make very suitable footwear. There was one interesting feature on the shore. There was some sort of 3-foot wide cement platform that jutted out six feet into the channel. It was about a hundred feet from the bridge, which was a bit farther than I thought would be optimum for a casting platform, but it was still notable.

With the water barely moving I made a call back to Long Island to check in with my wife and let her know that all was well and she wouldn't be hearing from me until the next day. While we talked, I had one ear listening for any busts under the bridge. There were none. There was only a slight breeze, so it was pretty easy to read the water. By the time I was off the phone, the reflection of the bridge lights on the water showed that a distinct rip line had formed on the ebb's down-current side of the bridge. It was time to fish.

I settled on a bunker-colored 7-inch Tsunami Swim Shad to start. I'm realistic and keep my expectations in check. Given that I was fishing for a species of fish I had never seen before, I would be happy to put in several hours for a hookup. It would take three casts. The hit was so hard and had come so soon that it caught me off guard. Before I could even react properly the fish was airborne and clearly visible in the bridge lights as it shook off my lure. It would be lucky to break 30 pounds, but it was a tarpon, and so early into my 5-day trip! I had never been so excited to lose a fish in my life. I had heard many times that only about one in ten hooked tarpon are landed, so there was no shame in losing my first, or the next four that I hooked on the first half of the ebb. Each one threw the hook on a jump.

It was well after midnight and I hadn't had a hit in a while. Cognizant of the fact that I wanted to be fishing a flat early in the morning, I gave it the "three more casts" announcement. Since my early days of fishing, this has been an announcement to the fish to do something to keep me there, but not actually allow me to catch something. On the second of three casts I leaned into a solid hit, and to my amazement, I was still connected to the fish on the instantaneous first jump. It wasn't a big

My first tarpon was a small one, but exciting nonetheless.

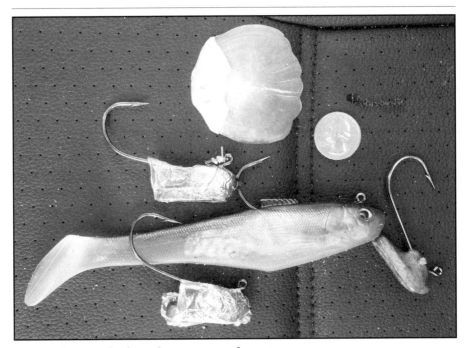

Wrecked swim shads and a tarpon scale.

fish, but I was as happy as could be when I pulled the 15-pounder in between two rocks and got my hand on its lower jaw. I had caught my first tarpon.

The next night was similar to the first, and I didn't hear or see a single splash either night. Apparently, the cold front that went through just prior to my arrival had put the fish off a bit. Still, I was doing OK, landing 3 of 14 hookups. These weren't the big tarpon I had come to the Keys for, but all juveniles in the 15- to 30-pound range.

Tuesday night was the last time I saw the temperature drop below 79 degrees, even in the middle of the night. It was in the mid-80s with strong sunshine during the day. By Wednesday night, I knew things were going to be different when I heard the first surface busts as the flood current began to weaken just after dark. It wasn't long before I was hooking, and promptly losing, big tarpon on the Tsunami 7-inch swim shads. These were the ones with the thinner chemically sharpened hooks. Unfortunately, the violent airborne headshakes of the tarpon were damaging the lures. At the rate they were ripping apart the shads, I knew I'd be out of them by the end of the third night and would have to switch to the Calcutta swim shads that I had brought with me. The problem was that I had tried the Calcuttas several times on earlier nights and had never been able to get the fish to hit them with the frequency that they hit the Tsunamis.

They say necessity is the mother of invention, and with the destruction of my last Tsunami, it was time to figure out a way to make the Calcuttas work. It was frustrating making cast after uninterrupted cast with the Calcuttas knowing that if I had more Tsunamis with me, I'd be hooking up. After going some time without a hit, I noticed the Calcutta blow out and pop to the surface soon after I ended one of my normal moderately fast retrieves and began to burn the lure back. Was my retrieve too fast for the Calcutta to handle the current? I decided to gradually start knocking the retrieve speed down to see if the lure would track better on a slower retrieve and maybe convince the fish to eat. As I dropped down to about two-thirds of the Tsunami retrieve speed, I found the sweet spot.

I stuck the first hit solid, and watched six feet of chrome shake in the air illuminated by the bridge lights. It sounded as if someone fell off the bridge when the fish touched down. The fish screamed to my right, up-current, and away from the bridge. The spool spun so fast that it warmed quickly from the friction on the drag washers as the fish made huge leaps away from me as it ran. Most jumping fish I had caught in my life would jump straight up and land where they exited the water. This tarpon was traveling through the air and landing more than ten feet from where it first broke the surface. Two hundred yards of line were gone in no time and I worried I might run out of line. This fish would dwarf my best tarpon, if I could land it. The fish finally settled down, and I was able to gain line slowly by pulling the rod back with my right arm while my left hand alternated between cupping the spool and taking two or three cranks on the reel handle. Twenty minutes into the fight, I had almost all of the line back, but the fish was now using the current to its advantage as it swam toward the bridge where I'd surely be cut off. The fish exploded next to a piling, grazing it in the process, and was spooked up-current. It was on, tiring, and I felt I had a fair chance of landing it. With the increasing current, I knew I had to bear down harder and pull the fish farther from the bridge. As I pulled it to within fifty feet of me, I nearly fell over backwards as the line broke. A close inspection showed the 50-pound-test braid frayed, likely when the fish was near the piling. This is as close as I would come this night, as I would land none of the twelve fish that I had hooked. The bite was on.

Thursday night I was dialed in with the Calcuttas. The fish were even more plentiful and the epic battle of the previous night played out four more times. There was the fish that I felt was close to landing until it broke brand new braid as it landed on a jump. I could only think that it cut the line with its gill plate, because I had bowed to the jump and definitely didn't apply enough pressure to break 50-pound-test braid. The next fish was on more than 15 minutes and still more than 100 yards away when the hook simply pulled. The next one was a heart-breaker, when after a battle that started with significant flood current remaining, ended early on the ebb only 20 feet away when the fish chafed through the 80-pound-test leader material. Being relatively inexperienced at fishing for tarpon, I had not had this happen before. The next fish was on for about 10 minutes, but was unmovable down-current of my position with hard flowing ebb current. It also parted the leader. In the two nights combined I managed to land none of the 22 hookups.

Friday was breezy and the ocean was too rough and messy for my daytime kayak fishing, so I found more sheltered water on the north side of the Overseas Highway and in the lee of one of the larger islands. Similar to the fishing I had experienced on the ocean side, I ended up having a ball with barracuda and toy sharks.

I needed to do some tackle shopping between the kayak trip and that night's tarpon trip. I found buying fishing tackle a little strange in the Florida Keys. If I was home on Long Island, I could buy good swim shads in at least four different stores within a few miles of my house, but I couldn't find any in the 50-mile stretch from Marathon to Key West because, as I was told by two tackle shop owners, "Those won't work here." Oddly enough, you could buy 100-pound-test leader material in the Winn Dixie grocery store, so that's what I did in preparation for my final night, and one last shot at a big tarpon before I left. I used an 80-pound-test SPRO barrel swivel, and the 100-pound-test leader material was so thick it barely passed through the swivel eye.

The night started off slow and quiet. I clung to hope on the rare surface splashes and single hookup with a "small" 30-pound class tarpon that spit the hook. Throughout the course of the week I had fished both up-current and down-current of the bridge. I was now positioned around

75 feet down-current, with the last of incoming water. I began to think back with satisfaction on my five days and nights of fishing and the intense jump-filled battles that I'd never forget. The day's fun flats wading for cudas was a nice way to finish it off if this last night wasn't going anywhere.

The rare moment of reflection was interrupted by a solid jolt and deep rod pulsations. The 6-foot-plus fish launched from the water directly in front of me, crashed about 15 feet down-current, and just kept going with the dying flood. I was thankful it was moving away from the bridge. I held on helplessly as it alternated between running and leaping until it finally stopped with my spool hot and over two thirds empty. Now in open and obstruction-free water, a tug of war ensued for the next 15 minutes while I gradually rock-hopped 30 feet down-current to the little cement platform that would allow me to fight the fish from a flat surface and several feet from the shore.

I gained a lot of line back as the current weakened, and finally slacked. This was the perfect scenario of fighting the fish with slow to no current. I had done the same the previous night with the first fish that broke the leader. After about 25 minutes the fish crossed from right to left in front of me, as it was pushed back to the bridge with the first trickle of the ebb. I applied as much pressure as I dared, understanding that if I couldn't bring it back to me soon, I would have no chance of moving its massive profile against the strengthening current. I didn't think it was near the bridge yet, but it suddenly leaped out of the water and grazed the same piling that the fish had frayed my line on two nights prior. Contact with the piling spooked the fish into changing direction back into the current, allowing me to recover some precious line. I had now fought enough tarpon to understand that each jump zapped energy, and I exploited that by pulling and cranking hard to get the fish back in front of me. The fight was now thirty minutes long.

The somewhat weakened fish was now in front of me and close, but we were in a standoff as it angled its immense body against the current. I felt a violent tug as the fish jumped so close that I was splashed when it hit the water. "Now or Never!" I shouted, as I leveraged the effects of the jump and pulled hard enough on the rod to turn its head toward me. With two more strained sideways sweeps of the rod, I grabbed the 100-pound-test leader and pulled the fish into the up-current corner formed by the small cement structure I was standing on and the rocks that lined the shore. With the rod in one hand and the leader in the other, I jumped into the waist-deep water beside the fish, released the leader, and grabbed the fish's lower jaw. Without breaking momentum, I lunged for the intersection of the wall with the shore rocks in water that was only two feet deep. With current pushing the fish against the cement wall and me pulling its head to the shore, I finally had control. I feared the fish thrashing the crap out of me, but it just wobbled back and forth a couple of times and came to rest. I did it!

I knew I had little time. As I've done with stripers many times, I grabbed my digital camera from the side pocket of my surf bag and sat it on one of two perfectly positioned rocks on the shore. It took three button pushes to commence a series of five photos. I cut the leader, stepped back with the fish, and let the camera do the rest. I needed only to hold the fish in front of the camera as the pictures were fired off at five-second intervals. In one more button push, I was able to confirm that the fish was reasonably framed. The fish was huge, and I wanted length and girth measurements for a weight calculation. I grabbed my leader spool, made a loop, and hooked it over the lower jaw of the fish while I ran the line straight back to the fork of the tail. I snipped that, stuffed it in my bag, and then ran another length of line around the midsection, just ahead of the dorsal fin. This was a little more difficult as the fish wobbled around for a few seconds before allowing me to get it right. There was only a jig hook where the swim shad used to be, and it popped out of the inside of the fish's mouth pretty easily. Less than two minutes had passed since leading the fish to shore. Reviving the fish was facilitated by the flow of the ebb current, which now had some force behind it. The fish regained its strength quickly and swam back into the channel.

I measured the length and girth leader segments the next day. The fish was 75 inches long with a 37-inch girth. The Bonefish and Tarpon Trust weight calculator converted that to 151 pounds. As of this writing, it remains the largest fish I've ever caught.

A tarpon with a calculated weight of 151 pounds landed from the shore of a Florida Keys channel.

CHAPTER 13
SPRING FLATS BLUEFISH SCARE

"I'm not going to make it back." That was the stark reality that set in when I began wading back to the shore of Peconic Bay and realized that the tide had risen much faster than I had anticipated. This was serious. A quarter-mile of 55-degree water separated me from the shoreline on this chilly and overcast mid-May morning. After 40+ years of making all kinds of fishing trips day and night from surf and boat, I had finally blown it. I was going to end up in the water. This was only my second season living on the North Fork, and my inexperience with the bay side had just caught up with me. I couldn't understand what had happened, since I didn't recall wading much deeper than my knees all of the way out, and I hadn't fished on the end of the bar for all that long. After all, it was a work morning and I didn't have all day. I had previously studied the area on Google Earth, but sand structure is known to change, and satellite imagery really only gives relative depth, not how many feet of water is actually over the structure. Many things raced through my mind, but I took some relief in knowing that I was definitely going to survive.

Despite the situation I put myself in, I'm an overly cautious fisherman. I even wear an inflatable PFD when jetty fishing. I always consider the worst-case scenarios and take steps to mitigate the potential for damage and injury and make sure I eventually get home alive. The incidental safety step taken on this trip was that I was wearing a neoprene surf top, specifically a Stormr Strykr. I say it was incidental because the jacket was chosen primarily for warmth, but I was fully aware of the safety value it offered should I end up swimming instead of standing. My friend, and perhaps the best fisherman I know, Joey Marino, put his Stormr Strykr to the test one November morning when he rolled his 18-ft Parker in the ocean off Moriches. He ended up in the cold water for several minutes until a nearby boat picked him up. He told me the jacket kept him floating and relatively warm.

My phone was left in the truck eliminating the option of calling someone to get me off the bar. The waterway was seldom traveled, so I knew I was on my own. I realized I could take my waders off, but I thought it best to just belt them tightly. They might eventually fill with water, but that water would be no heavier than the surrounding water, so it would not pull me under given the buoyancy of the jacket. Any water that got inside my waders would eventually warm slightly from body heat, so it was worth keeping them on for a little additional warmth. Hypothermia was a bigger threat in this situation than drowning.

The jacket would keep me afloat and the incoming current that put me in this situation would carry me toward a stretch of beach around a third of a mile away. I would end up cold, wet, embarrassed if seen, and very late for work. It was also my birthday, but not looking like a happy one. Why was I wading out more than a quarter mile into the bay in the first place? Big flats bluefish!

Almost every spring on both shores of Long Island, and I'm sure at other Northeast locations as well, big bluefish flood into the bays in the first couple of weeks of May. As opposed to the frenzied feeding that they're so well-known for, these blues are often found in large numbers finning and tailing on shallow 2- to 4-foot-deep flats. If the water is choppy, they're nearly impossible to find if you don't search for them by casting. These are some of the largest bluefish I'll encounter all season.

These fish can be incredibly picky at times, while at other times they'll happily crush topwater lures. This has led anglers who have observed these fish at times when they won't hit to conclude that they're on the flats to spawn. It's a logical conclusion considering that young-of-the-year snapper blues will appear in these same bodies of water a few months later, but that is not why they're there. Bluefish actually spawn on the open ocean, just like menhaden (bunker).

I don't have a good reason for why the blues are on the flats in May. Sometimes you'll see what looks like a triangle poking out of the water and not moving. That triangle is the tip of a big bluefish tail. If it was moving like a tailing southern redfish, I might think the fish was rooting out crabs, but that does not appear to be the case. Throw a plug near that stationary triangle and it is likely to spook the fish. These fish sometimes spit up well-digested bunker when I catch them, but hours spent on a flat full of bluefish might show just a handful of instances where I witness a surface attack.

It's remarkable that a cursory look at a flat full of big bluefish might show nothing but the appearance of fishless water. I have never seen gulls work these schools, which is further evidence that they're not chasing and injuring baitfish. I'll suggest one completely unsupported theory as to why these fish are choosing to quietly hang out in a few feet of water each May. These fish have just completed a long migration in relatively cold water. They may be seeking out the warmer flats to recharge a bit. Since they're not spawning and not actively feeding, it seems as good a guess as any. Because I don't know what motivates them, the only way I know to anticipate where they are is to check the places where I've caught them in previous seasons. I cast pencil poppers to see if they're present. It's always a thrill when I check water that I'm pretty sure is dead, only to have it erupt within my first couple of casts.

This particular morning started off as a striper trip a few minutes' walk from the flat. I had the end of outgoing water at first light and did well bucktailing a nearby channel. There were no bluefish there, but plenty of small to keeper size bass. I fished that tide down to the last drop and started walking back. Because the creek current lagged that of the surrounding area, there was already the first trickle of incoming water when I approached the flat. Fully aware of the potential for bluefish, I had my eyes peeled as I approached the edge of the sandbar that bordered the flat. At this stage of the tide, it had only a few inches of water over it. As I walked closer, I noticed something irregular on the otherwise glass-calm surface. At first I thought they were the tips of bunker tails, but then one of them moved. These were bluefish!

To get to the bar that bordered the flat, I needed to wade through a 150-ft wide trough of water up to my thighs. From having done this before I understood that this trough was the limiting factor in wade fishing these shallows. If I could come and go across that trough, I could fish the flat. Before wading out through what appeared to be the shallowest part of the trough, I made a mental note of a bush on the shore so that I would have a target on the return trip. Given the rising tide, I knew the trough depth was a constraint, but it was the very beginning of the incoming so I thought I should easily have ninety minutes of fishing. I suppose someone concerned about getting to work on time might actually carry a watch, but I didn't have one to time how long I spent on the bar. I was not planning to fish there long.

The 7 ½-foot rod that I bucktailed the bass with was rather perfect for 6-inch pencil poppers that had worked here the previous spring. Not wanting to spook the fins protruding from the water in front of me, I intentionally overcast them. The plug never made it to the fins as it was crashed multiple times before being pulled under to the sound of a screaming drag. This was one of those times that the quiet flats blues were anything but quiet when offered a plug.

I landed or lost a fish nearly every cast for the first thirty minutes, but the fish seemed to gradually move out, so I kept following. When the fishing slowed after about an hour, I saw subtle disturbances out near the end of the bar where I had never fished before. The water was a little deeper on the way out, but not enough to deter me from reaching a fresh pile of blues that ranged into the low teens. Screw work, it had been a long winter and it was my birthday and I was going to keep catching fish.

A spring flats bluefish hooked while wading well off the shore of Peconic Bay.

Catch I did, as all of the fish I spooked from in closer seemed congregated on the end of the bar. I played with them for about another 30 minutes, but when I was cut off for the second time, I decided I had caught enough and wasn't going to re-tie. With the depth of the trough on my mind, I located the bush that marked my landing point and headed straight for it. I guessed the trough would be a little more than waist deep when I got there and should be no trouble to cross. I was now 0.28 miles, or roughly 500 yards, from the beach as measured on Google Earth.

I plowed through knee-deep water for the first minute or so, but it was getting gradually deeper. When the water went over my thighs, I became concerned. I knew I was in serious trouble when I found myself in waist-deep water with easily 400 yards to go. If there was this much water out here, then the trough, which had significant current, would surely be over my waders. Due to the heavy overcast there was no opportunity for me to visually read nearby water depth. There was a gentle current, but the water was too high on the bar edge for me to see where it was. There was just a lot of water between me and the beach and it all looked the same. I did the only thing I could do – start wading toward the bush. I anticipated losing touch with the bottom at some point, at which time I'd swim in the direction of the current and deal with the result when I eventually hit land.

It was slow going for the next several minutes, but at least the depth had stabilized just over my waist. This was better than losing bottom way off the beach, but the depth only confirmed my belief that there was no way I'd make it across the trough. I continued to wade through belly-deep water for what seemed like an eternity, but in reality was probably ten minutes. With only a hundred yards left before reaching the beach, the bottom began rising slowly. In another minute the water was back at my thighs, and I realized I was likely out of danger. Crossing the trough was exactly as I thought it would be while I was fishing, with water a good six inches below the top of my waders. I was confused about what just happened, but relieved to be on the beach.

I drove straight to work, roughly an hour away. "Not now!" were the first words out of my mouth when I found a scientist waiting at my office door. It was a tone he wasn't accustomed to hearing from me, so he retreated while asking me to visit his office when I had time. My first order of business was to head straight for Google Earth on my office computer to try to understand what had just happened. I had explored many spots with satellite imagery when I moved to the North Fork, but I had missed an important detail with this one that was visible only from above. When observed from the beach, the edge of the bar appeared to run straight out. What could not be seen an hour plus into the rising tide on an overcast day was that the bar had a subtle curve near the end. I was busy watching and catching fish as I traversed this and there were no points of reference because I was so far out. My only concern was that I wouldn't wade into anything too deep. Because I moved out gradually while fishing, I never noticed the curve or that I had moved slightly parallel to the shore. When it was time to head for shore, I headed straight for the bush. I was then far enough off my original path that I ended up wading on the inside of the bar curve, and through water that was twice as deep as expected. At the time I attributed this to the rising tide, when in reality I had taken the wrong path back to shore.

It's easy to get distracted in the presence of fish, and that's what happened. I had never intended to wade out so far, and I failed to study the satellite imagery carefully enough to realize that a curved path was required to stay on the shallowest return path. These days I always carry a phone with me. If I had done so this trip, I could have used the Google Earth App to get me out of there the best way, or if I was in a life-threatening situation, I could call for help. Aside from the awesome fishing, the trip

A 16.5-pound bluefish that hit a Savage Gear Panic Pencil from the shore of Peconic Bay.

left me a bit frustrated. I try to be careful, but I still almost ended up in a bad situation. After 40+ years of fishing I was still making stupid mistakes. I didn't study the satellite imagery close enough, I didn't pay close enough attention to my path as I waded out, and I didn't have my phone. Take away any of these mistakes and I would have waded back the same way I went out and avoided the biggest scare I've ever had fishing. I guess one way to look at it is if that's the most dangerous thing that ever happens to me while fishing, then I've done OK. Even so, the lessons learned that chilly morning in May will stay with me until I'm in the old folks home watching *Seinfeld* reruns I can't remember.

CHAPTER 14
ALBIE EXPLOSION

"Only five more. That's all I need." I said to an angler friend as I passed him on a North Fork Long Island beach on a beautiful early November morning. The five I *needed* were False Albacore, aka Little Tunny, or as most anglers refer to them, albies. Ten years earlier I wouldn't have dreamed about saying "only five" to describe how many albies I was hoping to catch on a trip, but this was 2017, and the fishery had gradually exploded to the point that catch numbers in the double digits were commonplace. I had begun catching them six weeks earlier, and had enough big days that my season count stood at 295, all from the beach. Two hours later I released number 300, and hung up my albie gear for the season without making another cast. My logs show that the insanity started in 2015, a fall season highlighted by a trip where I beached 72 in one long 10 ½-hour casting session. I guess there's a little bit of obsession there, but at what point do you walk off the beach when they're hitting that well? This is my log notation from October 22, 2015.

So this was THE day. I almost didn't go considering yesterday, but saw just enough SW wind on the buoy, and given the good tide and the recent great fishing, I decided to make the drive. Thank God I did. I would have needed counseling if I missed this one. The ebb was good, not off the scale, but I guess excellent with 21 fish up until slack low, around noonish. I almost bailed for a half day, but moved farther into the cove for the flood and immediately started hooking up. The bite kept getting better as the wind increased to a pretty strong wsw crosswind and 2-3 foot waves. I think I might have used a #3 all day, but I know for sure that's what I used in the afternoon, and I just kept hitting them and didn't know when to stop. When I finally had enough, my count was an amazing 72 albies landed, and good luck to anyone wanting to beat that in one day.

That did seem at the time to be an unbeatable one-day catch, but twice during the 2017 run I probably could have topped it if I hadn't left the albies to go to another beach to catch stripers. In one instance I had 58 by 12:30 pm. Another day I had 55 by 11:30 am. Both days I found such good striper fishing in the afternoon that I didn't regret leaving the albies. Big number days like that helped put me in the position where I needed only five more to reach 300. My previous best season was in 2015 when I landed 223. The difference this time was that I now lived in Greenport, and very close to the action.

All of this was being done while working full time. I was an excellent employee most of the year, but my co-workers and management understood that for around six weeks in the fall, I would show up when the bite slowed and use vacation time in fractional days to make it fair. This was possible because I almost never went on real vacations. When people would ask me about that, I always said that I lived where people go to vacation, so I didn't need to go anywhere. Living in Greenport meant I started each day where the fish were and could conveniently assess the fishing and the conditions to decide whether to work, fish, or split my time between both. This was much trickier prior to 2017 when I would need to make a 40-minute drive east to fish, and then drive 50 minutes west to work. Few things in fishing are worse than making a long drive to find out the conditions are no good. What is worse is not making the drive because you think the water is dirty, only to find out while you're in work that the water's fine and the fish are hitting anything that moves.

Seasonal timing is a big variable. I've followed North Fork albie runs for nearly 20 years and understand them pretty well. I'll spell it out here, but will avoid mentioning specific access points as these are subject to change due to parking regulations. Consider the following to apply to the beaches along the roughly 15-mile stretch between Southold and Orient Point. Much of what I write here with respect to conditions will apply to False Albacore fishing in many other locations in the Northeast and beyond. I'll follow with gear and technique observations that are applicable everywhere.

There are actually two fall albie runs on Long Island's North Fork. The first starts around the middle of September when the fish move into the Sound and spread as far west as Huntington and beyond. In contrast to what I consider the main run, this one is inconsistent and the good bites are hard to predict. At this time the fish are often visible thrashing the surface while they feed on small bay anchovies. As is usually the case when albies are on these baitfish, the fish can be very picky. You'll sometimes see the fish set up in a rip and show themselves periodically, but they don't appear to be on the move east or west. Compared to fish caught in mid- to late-October, these fish fight harder pound-for-pound, although I've never landed any of the larger 10-pound-plus fish in September. I've had a few good sessions on this early run, but I don't expend a lot of energy on it because of the unpredictability. Some years this run doesn't materialize enough for there to be decent fishing. In the years that it does, it's usually a steady thing, with maybe a dip at the end of the month. The real fun starts roughly somewhere between October 7th and 15th with what I call *The Exodus Run*.

You can usually tell how good this second run will be in the first days of October by checking the boat fishing reports between Port Jefferson and Huntington. If there are good catches being made in areas such as Cranes Neck, Middlegrounds, and Eatons Neck, then hold on, the North Fork has great fishing ahead. I've always thought of it as the exodus run because it's when all of those False Albacore that are spread in that large and wide middle to western section of the Sound, as well as the ones between Port Jefferson and Mattituck, will make a run for it and leave the Sound as the water temperature drops. When they do, they inevitably end up colliding with the North Fork beaches on the way out. When it will start is highly dependent on the weather. I've seen exodus runs start as early as the first week of October, and I've seen them end as early as the third week of October in unseasonably cold weather. This was exactly the case in 2009 when I set the New York State False Albacore record with a 16.4-pounder caught from the shore on October 17th as the run was ending early. That record stood until 2021, when an 18-pounder was caught by an angler offshore fishing in the ocean. The largest albies I've seen landed, and I've seen thousands, have typically come at the end of the run.

It might be hard to imagine the words "dependable" and "albies" being used together in the same sentence, but in the typical years when albies move into the Sound, it's close to a sure thing that they'll be caught from several North Fork beaches during the last two weeks in October. This is especially true any day with a stiff onshore wind. If you look at a map of Long Island Sound and imagine all of those False Albacore spread between Mattituck and Huntington moving east with purpose as water temperatures drop, you can see how they'll concentrate and intersect the North Fork shoreline as it curves out into the Sound.

Unlike albie fishing at other times and in most other areas, this is primarily a blind-cast fishery. It's not uncommon for a couple of dozen anglers to collectively beach a couple of hundred albies while the fish are only rarely seen busting on the surface until they're behind someone's lure. At times when the waves are big enough and the water is clear enough, you might see schools of them in the wave faces all speeding west to east. When I'm casting, I pay much more attention to anglers to my west than ones to my east. When I see bent rods to the west, it's time to be extra ready because some fish will be passing in front of me on the next cast or two. Sometimes you can actually watch a school of albies swim by without ever seeing them just by watching the progression of hooked up anglers from west to east. No matter when I'm targeting albies, my approach is to set up on an area known to be on their

Albies often fight hard all the way to the beach.

migration route and just keep blind casting. Even if you see them boil up some distance down the shore, it's pointless to try and chase them. You're much better off maximizing the time your lure is running through the strike zone.

Like any fishery, some days are better than others. I'll describe what I want to see for good North Fork fishing, but much of this applies to other locations as well, especially regarding water quality. Weather and water conditions are everything. You must have clean water – period. If it's even a little dirty, the fish will stay farther off the beach where it's cleaner. The best wind on the North Fork is a stiff onshore between 15 and 20 mph. If you have that wind in your face with clean water in the second half of October, you can be almost guaranteed that albies will be screaming drags on several of the beaches. Keep in mind that the North Fork has a very irregular shoreline, so a cross wind on one beach will be right in your face at another nearby beach. Generally, a wind direction close to Northwesterly is ideal. Anything between WSW and WNW and more than 25 mph will dirty the water and shut down the fishing. This happens because there is a very long fetch in that direction. If you draw a line at 260 degrees from the tip of Rocky Point in East Marion, that line will stay over water for 70 miles. That's a long way for waves to build, and that's what they'll do on those strong westerlies. When the resulting ocean-like waves crash on the North Fork beaches, they'll stir things up and dirty the water. The good news is that the water clears in less than a day when the wind lets up, and there's often good fishing for bass, blues, and albies just as the water clears. When the wind blows from the NNW, which is directly across the Sound, the fetch is only 9 to 12 miles depending on what beach you're fishing. On those winds the waves simply don't have enough distance to build to heights large enough to dirty the water, unless the wind is stronger than 40 mph. The best time of day for albie fishing is kind of interesting. I've started catching them as early as just before sunrise, but I've rarely done well on the other end of the day near sunset. The best hours for me have been between sunrise and noon.

There are rare years when there is almost no run at all. When Hurricane Irene made landfall near NYC as a Tropical Storm in 2011, its path took it inland where it dumped enough rain to cause severe flooding. The muddy debris-filled rivers of Connecticut drained into

Long Island Sound for at least the following week, into the beginning of September. From the top of the high bluff in Wading River I saw a lot of brown water and floating tree debris. The timing of this dirty water influx coincided with when the albies should have been going into the Sound. They didn't that year, and I've always blamed Irene. 2020 was also a particularly poor year, and because I didn't see any environmental causes, I've just assumed it was because it was my first albie year in retirement when I would have had all of the time in the world to pursue them!

I've often said that artificials catch fish either through imitation or by obscuring the fact that they're really just a piece of metal, wood, or plastic. The challenge with False Albacore is that they have very keen eyesight, and if the water is calm and clean, they do an excellent job of spotting fakes as they ignore lures even while blitzing baitfish. If you're trying to fool them by imitation alone, your offering better be rather exquisite and of the same size as the bait they're feeding on. This is why fly-casting anglers with very realistic looking small flies can often out-fish anglers with spinning gear when the primary forage is small anchovies, which is often the case in Long Island waters in September.

My approach is to use high quality shiny lures, and obscure them so the fish can't get a very good look. You cannot out-reel a False Albacore, so I burn my lures at top speed and skip them across the surface of the water. This leads to explosive surface hits that are as exciting as the actual battles. Because almost all of my albie fishing is done from shore, and good casting distance is often important, I throw only metal. If you walk into a tackle shop and look for albie lures, you're likely to find three different types. Some, such as Deadly Dicks, are all stainless-steel. Others are lead jigs that have very attractive finishes. You probably wouldn't know they were lead unless you picked one up and felt the weight. Then there are the epoxy jigs. These are often the prettiest and most realistic looking lures, but I never use them. I am fully aware that they catch fish and are favored by many skilled albie anglers. What I don't like about them is their low density, which simply put, means they're larger than the other lures of equivalent weight. This means they don't cast as far, and they're barely in the water when retrieved at the high speeds that I like.

If I could have only one albie lure, it would be a green #2 Deadly Dick. Many anglers refer to this as a 2-ounce, but that's not the case. A #1 Deadly Dick weighs 0.8 ounces, a #2 is 1.3 ounces, and a #3 is 1.7

ounces. These lures cast far and do a good job of splashing up the surface and throwing off a lot of flash. If I have a stiff onshore wind, or need a ridiculously long cast, I'll go for the denser lead-based lures. A 2-ounce Hogy Heavy has a small profile that is often the right size for the fish, but can cut into a 20-knot wind when needed. The only challenge with this lure is that it is difficult to splash on the surface when it's calm. It's fine in a chop, and one of those very productive sessions of beaching over fifty albies in one morning came on this lure. In September, when the fish are likely to be feeding on small anchovies, the 1.25-ounce Hogy Heavy or 1-ounce Hogy Peanut are small profile lures that look like the real thing and cast a long distance.

I take very good care of my albie lures, making a point to rinse them in fresh water after use. If you don't do this, the stainless Deadly Dicks will lose their nice shiny finish. I also do it to keep the hooks from rusting. I'm almost superstitious about my leader material, and use a roughly 30-inch leader of clear 20-pound-test Seaguar Blue Label Fluorocarbon. I'm sure there are other brands of Fluorocarbon that work just fine, but I like the way Seaguar knots and it has worked so well for me that I don't want to mess with it. As mentioned, the most intense bites I've experienced have been in onshore winds of 15 to 20 mph. It probably helps to push the fish closer to shore, but under those conditions the North Fork beaches I fish will have waves around 2 feet. That's perfect, because the chop makes it hard for the fish to get a good look at the lure, but it's not so rough that the water dirties.

I mentioned clear Fluorocarbon in the previous paragraph. I don't know why they even make pink Fluorocarbon, but I wouldn't touch the stuff for this kind of fishing. A few years ago, an angler next to me was having trouble getting any fish to hit his jig, while I hooked up every few casts. We were both throwing #2 Deadly Dicks and burning them in on the surface. He finally asked me out of frustration what I thought he might be doing wrong, and I immediately asked him about his leader material. This was a flat calm day, and under those conditions a visible leader will turn the fish off. He told me it was 20-pound-test, like mine, so I walked over to look at his lure and rigging. It was then I noticed he was using pink Fluorocarbon. "This is your problem," I told him. He immediately protested telling me how many he caught the day before with the same leader material. I was on the beach the day before, and knew it was a rather rough day with fish that were much less picky. Rather than debate him, I gave him one of my leaders. To his credit, he re-rigged with it, and it took only a few casts for a fish to commit. After that he caught at nearly the same pace that I did.

I do not tie my leaders directly to the braid, but instead go through a high quality 100-pound Tsunami Centro or 80-pound SPRO barrel swivel. The swivel offers what I feel is a stronger connection between the two different line materials, but even if you argue that some braid to Fluorocarbon knots are just as strong, I want that swivel to help reduce line twist. Because I'm reeling fast, I'm making many casts each session. Burning some tins on the surface may cause them to spin for short periods of time, and you'll be able to see this twist if you look carefully at your spool. It's one of the reasons I favor Deadly Dicks. These come with a large shiny barrel swivel at the front of the jig. My insistence on rinsing these lures after each use assures that the swivels will stay in fine working order. I add chrome swivels to all of my albie lures that don't already come with them, and I tie direct from the leader to the lure without going through a clip.

I've mentioned my high-speed retrieves. There have been a handful of rare occasions when I saw myself being out-fished because I was reeling too fast. Keep in mind I'm thinking of three trips over the course of hundreds, but there was no doubt that I needed to make an adjustment to maximize my catch. All of these instances were late in the run when the water started getting cold. These were calm days, the fish were relatively close, and I noticed that the anglers throwing the Hogy Epoxy jigs and retrieving them below the surface were getting more hookups than I was. I notice pretty quickly when others are catching and I'm not, so it didn't take long for me to see what I needed to adjust. In each case I went to a #1 Deadly Dick and reduced the retrieve speed. I'm so used to reeling at top speed that it actually took some discipline to reel slower, but that corrected the problem. It's always smart to pay attention to anglers around you to see what's working and what's not

I rarely address etiquette, but will do so here for anglers who are new to catching these fish. When you hook up, pressure the fish and get it in. This will keep crossed lines to a minimum and give the best chance at a healthy release. I once watched a guy playing with his cell phone

Deadly Dick lures are a favorite among many False Albacore anglers.

while an albie screamed line off his reel – line that then tangled a couple of nearby anglers. Because these fish are strong runners and often feed in current, it is sometimes unavoidable that a fish will explode down the shoreline and in front of other anglers. Pay attention to those around you, and hold your cast if necessary to avoid crossing a line attached to a hooked fish. The first couple of times that you hook an albie from shore, you can certainly be excused for how much line might end up off your spool and possibly down the shoreline in a very short time. That's to be expected until you've gained a little experience with them. After that you'll learn how to pull with your rod parallel to the water as opposed to overhead, and you'll find yourself beaching them pretty quickly. You'll know you did it right when your fish hits the beach with its tail thrashing rapidly.

I find 7- to 8-foot medium power rods matched with 4000 size spinning reels to be ideal for these fish and the lures used to catch them. The tin skipping that many of us do for albies can be tiring because you need to crank very fast to achieve the speed to skip the tin, obscure the lure, and get the fish to crash it. High gear ratio reels make this a lot easier. The Penn Clash 4000 with a gear ratio of 6.2:1 pulls 35 inches of line per turn of the reel handle. A Van Staal VR50 with its 6.3:1 gear ratio pulls 37 inches of line. At one time I would have referred to these as "high speed." Then came the Penn Clash II 4000HS, where the "HS" stands for "high speed." These reels have a 7.0:1 gear ratio and pull an amazing 44 inches of line per turn of the reel handle. That is truly a high speed for a 4000 size reel. The speed of this reel has spoiled me because I no longer have to work so hard to keep the lures flying across the water's surface. I have not surveyed the market to see what other manufacturers are offering, but I can highly recommend the Clash II HS reels for albies because of their speed, light weight, braid friendliness, and smooth drag. The reel should be filled with line, because if you hook into an albie heavier than 10 pounds, you might need a lot of line to stop it. When fishing beaches with rocks, try to stay well up-current of any potential cutoffs, as once an albie gets going with the current, it's hard to stop. Besides wanting a high gear ratio for albies, I also want a reel with a slow oscillation speed for the purposes of good line management and reduced wind knots.

No matter what species you pursue with a spinning reel, the reel's oscillation speed is worth understanding. It was False Albacore fishing however that drew my attention to this reel characteristic. I use a lot of Penn reels, having grown up with them as I expect many anglers my age have. Reels from all manufacturers have gone through many upgrades and transformations since I first began surfcasting with a green Penn, and what I'll write about here applies to numerous brands of reels. I'll write about Penn models because that's what I use for albies.

Because I'm reeling very fast with a high gear ratio reel, I'm making nearly three casts per minute. For a three-hour casting session I might make nearly 500 casts if I don't get interrupted by fish. If you've ever watched me albie fish, you'll notice I don't take breaks to BS with people or to rest. I just keep casting. Thankfully, I'll probably be interrupted at least several times and get to fight some fish. If you cast lures on spinning reels with braided line, you know what a wind knot is. Wind knots are more frequent when there are instances of slack or little tension on the line during the retrieve. You're unlikely to experience wind knots if you're fishing something like a bucktail in current because that produces constant tension on the line. Skipping a tin on the water's surface provides very inconsistent tension to the line going on the spool, thus increasing the chance of a knot flying off the spool on the cast. Because my best albie catching is done with a stiff onshore wind, the chances of the line blowing up on a cast are further increased. When casting hard with a metal lure, those knots often result in a snapped line and a lost lure. This also results in the loss of braid, and you want your spool kept full both for line capacity on a long run as well as for reduced cast friction for long casts. At $25-$30 per 300-yard spool, line loss can get pretty expensive. Add to this the frustration of dealing with a line knot while you can hear the screaming drags of nearby anglers, and you can understand easily why every single one of the hundreds of casts made in an albie session needs to be trouble-free.

Many years ago I used Penn SS reels, and once the braid was broken in a bit, the casting was acceptably trouble-free. However, each season I made a point to make an albie trip earlier than I thought there would be any around just so I could condition the line. I eased into the casting, and didn't start gunning for long distance until I was fairly confident that I wouldn't get jolted by a knot wrapping a guide on the cast. I used well-worn lures on these trips just in case I snapped one or more off.

I'm not sure what year the Penn Clash reels hit the market, but I was immediately drawn to their lighter weight, which would help reduce fatigue on those 500-cast trips. The first time I used one to break in the line, I was surprised that there was no break-in period. The line behaved well from the beginning of the first trip, and throughout the albie run of that year. Around the same time, I bought a Penn Battle, but it wasn't as braid friendly and I stopped using it for albies. Fortunately, it made a great bass reel at a good price, so it wasn't wasted money. I stuck with the Clash for albies, and felt I had the ultimate albie reel as it was lightweight, smooth as silk, and had an exceptional drag.

At some point while corresponding with a Penn product developer, I mentioned how well braided line behaved with the Clash compared to my older SS and Battle, and he explained that the Clash and the Conflict II were Penn's slow oscillation reels. Oscillation speed refers to how fast the spool goes up and down when you turn the reel handle. The slower the oscillation, the closer together the line wraps are on the spool. If you look at the line lay on a spool of a slow oscillation reel, the stack of line is going to look smoother. Reel manufacturers usually cite casting distance as the major advantage to the slow oscillation, because that smoother spool creates less friction as the line comes off on the cast, therefore resulting in greater casting distance. While I've only heard a brief mention of reduced wind knots on slow oscillation reels, I can tell you without a doubt that this is a huge advantage when albie casting. It saves lures, line, lost time, and ultimately catches you more fish.

So why aren't all spinning reels slow oscillating? There's a liability in laying the line wraps more parallel to each other in that braid can cut into the spooled line under heavy pressure. Standard oscillation spinning reels have a slightly more crisscrossed line lay that prevents this from happening. This allows for tighter drags and greater pressure applied to lines without the worry of the line digging in. The very first time I ever used braided line, I buried it into the spool on the first hookup. You do that once, and after that you make sure you spool your line very tightly so that it never happens again. That's the way it went for me. Even with the slower oscillating reels, I've never had an issue with the line digging in, and I use as tight a drag as possible without having to worry about line breakage. If you have a "long cast" reel, it likely has a tall spool and a slow oscillation.

The best braid to use is a moving target due to near constant new offerings from the line manufacturers. I'll state my preference for the time this book was written. For the demanding albie application, you want a smooth 8-strand braid. I've used Daiwa J-Braid 8-strand since it came out because it's been strong, long-casting, and trouble-free on the Clash reels. I expect that J-Braid Grand is just as good, as I've used it for other applications. I use Berkley X9 for fluke jigging because it's the smoothest and thinnest line I've fished with. I tried it on the Clash II HS for albie casting and it performed well. There are undoubtedly other fine choices out there. I avoid the 4-strand braids because they're not as smooth and therefore reduce casting distance when compared to the 8-strand braids of the same manufacturers. That said, for striper fishing in rocky areas where you are going to inevitably have fish rubbing your line on boulders, I can't imagine a tougher line than Spiderwire Stealth, a 4-strand braid that I've used for many years.

The main attraction to albie fishing is an obvious one – nothing you can hook from the Northeast surf on a regular basis will smoke line off your spool faster than a False Albacore. The light payloads that catch these fish lend themselves well to being delivered with medium-power 7- to 8-foot rods that are comfortable to use, and the fish will fight you hard right to the shore. It's probably what drew me to albies in the first place, but I appreciate that catching them consistently and in good numbers requires skill and close attention to tackle details. There are days where they will seem to hit anything shiny that you speed through the water, but it's more often the case that the same anglers on the beach will keep hooking up over and over while others can't get a touch. What more could you ask from a fish?

I guess you could wish that it was good eating. False Albacore are widely considered inedible. Sometime early in life I mistook the first one I saw for a tasty green bonito. You make that mistake one time. I should have realized my error when I cut the fish and saw nothing but dark meat, but no, I proceeded to broil it and take a few bites. I've had people tell me they've enjoyed eating albies that were promptly bled and iced, but that is not the norm. The silver lining in the poor taste is that there is no commercial market and only the release mortality of recreational anglers to account for humans' impact on the stock. That's fine with me, as it leaves more albies to chase down my lures!

The 16.4-pound False Albcore that held the New York State record from 2009-2021.

CHAPTER 15
SPOOKED

I'll start this chapter with another writer's words, as they were responsible for filling an inexplicable gap in my surfcasting arsenal. This important tool wasn't added to my surf bag until 2019, and so wasn't included in my otherwise exceptionally thorough *Striper Pursuit* book. I remain extremely proud of that book, with my only regret being that it does not have a chapter on spook lures. This could be considered the missing chapter of that book. If you're a hardcore New England surfcaster, you might scratch your head over this, but I'll defend myself later. These are the words of Jerry Audet, whose name you might recognize from his writings in numerous fishing publications. Keep in mind this was an informal email, and not like the finely polished prose normally published under his name.

"So do you ever use a spook lure? Like a doc or a daddy mac lure style, or even a wood one? I ask because I was just at [location withheld] and casting a pencil for 10 minutes with no hook ups and then first cast with the spook and I hooked into a mother of a fish. Attached is the photo of what it did to the split ring (only one hook on this plug) because it got on a rock (I think) and it was a jumbo fish- that's a 100lb split ring that I put on myself. I then got broken off next cast after replacing the hook by a fish of equal size, then put on my only remaining spook and got broken off again. Back to the pencil, not a hit- eventually landed a high-teens on a glide bait. This is not a-typical for me- the spook often out fishes a pencil, although I admit I don't fish during the day a ton (or rather, rarely). They cast as far as a pencil, or very close, especially the daddy mac is a great casting plug with just a single hook (this was actually my first time using it, I have used the "doc" for years). Just a thought."

Anyone familiar with my work probably has no trouble believing that I own more than a thousand surf plugs. They are everywhere and on every flat surface in my basement, office, and garage. I haven't had to buy one in more years than I can remember. Years ago when I walked the shoreline I would scour the wrack line for lost plugs. Now when I'm on the beach I'm afraid to look down because I might accidentally find another, and have to stuff it in my bag. At the time I received Jerry's email, not one of these plugs was a large spook. I was aware of them, but other than at fishing shows, had only ever seen two in my life. Both were on the rods of fly boat guides who don't hesitate to speed from Long Island's North Fork to southern New England. Not once had I ever seen a surfcaster use one. A tackle distributer who deals with spook plugs told me when I finally inquired about them "We sell them in bulk to the Rhode Island and Mass. area, but seldomly in NY/NJ." If you're a New Englander wondering how it is that I didn't start using these plugs thirty years earlier, my first excuse will be that they were not even close to popular in my region. In fact, I had to order my first ones from Rhode Island.

I know Jerry is an intelligent guy who fishes very hard. He's one of the very few people who could suggest that I buy some more $20+ plugs and I would just take his word for it and order some sight unseen. I was intrigued by his account of fish that were ignoring pencils but clobbering spooks. I do a lot of pencil popper fishing, and it got me thinking about giving the fish something different to look at. I immediately checked J&H Tackle's website, and saw that Josh didn't carry any large spook plugs (he does now). Although Josh himself isn't a surfcaster, several very good ones work there, including a surf guide, and the store was otherwise well-stocked with surf lures. I knew the next fastest way to get these plugs was to place an order with Saltwater Edge. Stuff arrives from there so fast that I swear Peter must drive the packages to the New London Ferry right after the orders are placed.

Casting distance was a big concern. I knew the 9-inch would be the plug I'd want to put in front of fish, but the better-casting 7-inch would be the one that I might actually reach some fish with. I ordered two 7-inch "Lil' Doc" plugs, and soon after hitting the *Complete Order* button read an article on how the 7s don't have the fish pulling power of the 9s. Oh well. I ordered the 7-inch plugs the night I got Jerry's email, and they were at my house in less than 48 hours. "These will cast as well as a loaf of bread," was my original reaction. One went in the bag. The other went in a draw full of new plugs, as I reasoned I'd probably never need it.

The morning after receiving the plugs I ended a dawn trip by taking two casts with the spook out of curiosity. It was well past the time I was likely to get a hit, and mostly I wanted to see how it cast and if could put action on it. My only previous experience with a spook was throwing much smaller Heddon Spook Juniors for snook in Florida. The casting distance wasn't quite as bad as I imagined, but it wasn't even close to the distance I got with my pencils, which had been selected carefully for their ability to cast far and still work well. Nevertheless, I concluded that the spook went far enough to reach some fish. The real test would come that evening.

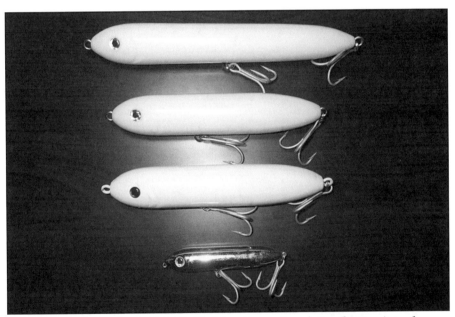

Spook Plugs from the 3 ½-inch Heddon Super Spook Jr. (bottom) to the 9-inch Musky Mania Doc (top).

I have several places where I pencil bass depending on tides and wind direction. This particular evening I was fishing a spot where the few fish that might be around tend to scatter over the area a bit, so it pays to start by fan casting. I spent around 25 minutes sweeping the water with a pair of pencils that had been producing fairly well, and elicited only one faint swirl. Subsequent casts over the spot yielded nothing, so I made a mental note of where I saw the swirl before moving on to the rest of the area that offered potential in casting range.

I referred to the saying that "fish swim" in Chapter 7. Anglers who subscribe to that way of thinking might assume that the fish that swirled the plug would be long gone ten minutes later, but I don't think that way if the fish aren't actively migrating. I believed that fish was still there, and I was pretty sure I could cast beyond it with the spook. I know this is not very forgiving, but my idea of trying a new plug means it gets two casts before landing back in the bag. I would relax this if I thought I would benefit, but my reasoning is that two casts are enough to get the attention of a fish in calm water, and if I don't get at least a look, I'll go back to what I know works and try the test lure some other time.

The water was glass-calm and very clear. I've said and written many times that you get a fish to hit an artificial either through imitation or by obscuring what the offering really is. The pencil popper is a good example of a lure that works by obscuring itself with surface splashing. It can be a beat up piece of wood, but if you tear up the water's surface with it so that all they see is an injured meal, the plug can be a killer. The spook isn't meant to work this way, but rather it should swim in a wide zig-zag pattern. This lure would have to imitate a wounded baitfish so well that a fish would eat it in daylight in calm, clear water.

After clipping the "Lil Doc" on for its first real test, I dragged it through the water with a few rod pulls to convince myself I could put action on it. I understood that this was a difficult evaluation with only a few feet of line hanging off the rod. I knew enough to know that the plug should glide a bit on its own after each pull if I allowed some slack in the line. The plug was almost certainly destined to end up back in the bag in two casts. Nonetheless, I wasn't catching, and it wasn't that special time right after sunset when fishless water sometimes comes to life. This was more like the time when you wonder why you came to the beach so early. Still, I imagined there was at least one faintly interested fish just to my left, and hopefully within spook range. Sometimes when you tell a story, it's easy to remember things in a way that don't match what really happened. I have what transpired on video, so there's no chance of that here, right down to how many seconds each fish visually stalked the plug.

The first cast touched down with a big loud splash, as if a seagull had just dropped an adult bunker from the sky. It took every ounce of restraint I had to not work it like a pencil popper, yet the video still looks like I'm working a pencil. I know there was a difference here, as I was not popping it, and I was allowing slack after each pull. I was just tugging on it at too high a frequency. Around 10 seconds in, an unmistakable swirl appeared behind the plug. Interpreting this to mean I was doing something right, my twitches and short slack pauses became more deliberate. I didn't know what else to do as the swirls progressed to a series of boils, followed by blowups, until 17 seconds after the initial swirl, the fish forgave my awkwardness with the plug's presentation and finally ate the lure. It was the longest 17 seconds of my fishing season. This fish had no doubt seen two of my pencils without showing much interest, but couldn't resist the spook in my inexperienced hands. Holy crap! This was an otherwise unnoteworthy low 20-pound class fish that I would never forget. But had I just gotten lucky?

On my fourth cast, recalling my snook plugging, I switched to retrieving with the rod held parallel to the water. My rod sweeps became less frequent and more deliberate to increase the side-to-side zig-zagging. My fifth cast produced another fish, which was followed by two others before they stopped hitting around 30 minutes after sunset. The last fish, a mid-teen, spent an incredible 21 seconds behind the plug before eating it! It was as if the plug was so powerful that the fish just couldn't leave it despite my imperfect retrieve!

I posted a video of this trip soon afterward, and it wasn't long before I heard through a third party that a local fly guide wasn't happy that I publicized the plug. Fly guides use these plugs to draw stripers near the boat and within casting range of their fly-fishing clients. I go through great lengths to protect spots, but I see no reason to hide techniques and lures. The thought of a "secret lure" seemed absolutely silly to me, but apparently it was a thing with regards to fishing big spooks for stripers, as was supported by a 2017 piece in *On the Water*. In that article, "Secret" Striper Plug: Musky Mania Doc, the writer extoled the virtues of the big spooks for coaxing large picky stripers into eating. He concluded the article by writing that the secret had actually been out for years, which I interpreted as his way of defending himself from any accusations of giving away the *secret*. Sure enough, the first comment on the online version of the article was "Some of us make a living with these, so **** You for sharing our secret." I'm not sure if that commenter was serious, but if nothing else, the article made me feel a little better about taking so long to learn about the plug.

Jerry was right on the money about the plug, except for his statement about it casting almost as far as a pencil. I can cast a pencil nearly twice as far as a 7-inch Lil Doc spook, and the 9-inch version casts even worse. That's a shame, because if you can get that 9-inch on the fish, I don't know of any better spooks. It's the plug of choice for most of those fly casters trying to raise bass for their clients. The problem is that I can't catch fish that I can't reach, and that played into my search for longer-casting spooks.

The first one I came across was the 6.5-inch Jigging World Spook, sold by Tackle World in New Jersey. Within two hours of the mailman delivering that plug, I was beaching 20-pound class stripers with it hours before sunset. It was that good. At 3.4 ounces it's a little heavier than the 2.6-ounce Lil Doc, and even out-weighs the longer 9-inch Doc by 0.4 ounces. It casts farther than the Lil Doc by a significant margin, yet the action remains persuasive enough for stripers to climb all over it. Its only downside is that if the plug swings back into a current of significant strength, it will dive below the water and lose the all-important wake on

A bass that hit a Dark Matter Astro Spook.

the water's surface. That said, the first cow I caught on the plug, a 34-pounder, grabbed the plug when it was nowhere in sight because the current had pulled it under.

The fatter and heavier 7-inch "Astro Spook" introduced by J&H Tackle under their Dark Matter brand in 2021 caught me by surprise. My first impression based on handling the 3.7-ounce plug left me skeptical that it could be cast easily or far, and I was concerned that the slightly larger diameter of the plug would degrade the desired side-to-side motion. I was wrong on all accounts. This turned out to be the longest casting spook in my bag. The wider body just meant a bigger meal for the stripers, and the action was phenomenal. It also did a good job of staying on the surface in current. With four colors offered, including chrome and the ever-popular bone, these plugs pushed most of the other spooks out of my bag. The "bunker" color looks like it was conceived by someone who had never seen a real bunker before. Nevertheless, the fish like something about that color and it's become one of the most productive spooks in my bag.

The key to getting a spook plug to do its thing is to allow a little slack after each rhythmic pull of the rod. I find it best to hold the rod side-armed when fishing a spook, as opposed to the traditional rod butt between the legs vertical orientation. This is awkward with an 11-foot rod, OK with a 10-footer, but I find it best with a 9-footer. This fits my fishing style just fine because, with the exception of rough ocean surf and inlet fishing, I prefer 9-footers for most of my surf fishing. My first spook fishing was with the 10-foot Lamiglas GSB101LS. I switched to the 9'2" J&H Dark Matter Skinner rod when that became available in 2020. That rod's sweet spot is 1 to 3 ounces, but given its moderate action it can handle heavier payloads to allow for casting large eels. I fish 6000-size reels spooled with 30-pound-test braid on both of these rods. With the rod tucked under the arm and held out to the side, it's easy to put rhythmic sweeps on the plug while watching it zig-zag across the surface. I find it much easier to react to and stick fish with the 9-footer than with the 10-footer, but the 10-footer is certainly doable. Fishing an 8-footer side-armed would be even more comfortable, but it would have to be a little stiff to handle casting the spook weight range.

In addition to the casting distance challenge, these plugs have not worked well for me in rougher water. I use them primarily in calm to

A nice bass that hit a 7-inch Lil' Doc Spook.

moderate surf, and appreciate a smooth water surface for the plug to leave a visible wake on. As is probably no surprise, these are difficult lures to cast into a stiff wind. They work well at night, making them the perfect lure to fish during the transition in and out of darkness. I tend to fish them interchangeably with pencils, and often start sessions with them and switch to pencils to cover more water after I think I've exhausted the potential in spook casting range.

I was so excited after my first evening fishing the big spook that I found it hard to sleep that night. When you've fished the beach for over forty years, it's rare to learn such an important lure that you've overlooked. It reminded me of the 9-year-old kid that I had taught how to jig for fluke one day the previous summer. After catching a couple of nice ocean fluke with his newly learned technique, he said to me "I feel like a whole new fisherman!" After catching fish on these plugs, I felt the same way.

The spook and pencil fishing has me on the Long Island Sound beaches a lot every season. I've been fortunate enough to live within walking distance of the Sound most of my life, while enjoying nearly 30 years of 4-wheel-drive access there, and a lifetime of kayak and boat access. Between the beach, boat, and kayak fishing, along with diving the waters since I was a teenager, I thought I had a good understanding of what lurked beneath its waters. I was in for an awakening.

Photo by Bill Moulton

CHAPTER 16
SHARK!

It started with an email. *"So this might be the most bizarre report you get from me, but it 100 percent happened. This evening penciling my buddy casted out while I wasn't looking and started freaking out because he said a big shark was waking behind his plug. He said easy 10ft shark. I was skeptical. He said he saw the dorsal and back fin clear as day do an S-type wake. I said OK not impossible. 10 casts later the shark came up on my plug and I saw it clear as day. This was a big shark. It had a very dark back and swam very lazy behind the plugs. What do you make of this? No bass BTW."*

The email was from an experienced fisherman, named Billy, who puts his time in on both the North and South Shore beaches. I had 100% confidence in the truthfulness of his report. Had he been fishing an ocean beach, especially Montauk, his account wouldn't have been at all surprising. Every summer, enough sharks show in the ocean surf that they are worthwhile targeting, and a fair number of surfcasters do just that in the absence of a reasonable chance of catching quality stripers during the doldrums. This report however came from a North Shore beach in Southold, well west of Orient Point. In all of my years being near Long Island Sound waters, I had never seen a shark. I recall reading of a couple of sightings in the 70's, and a friend told me he caught one in Huntington in the 60's. The only photographic evidence of Sound sharks I had ever seen came two weeks earlier. The first occurrence was at Iron Pier Beach in Jamesport, when a local fisherman recorded video of a shark swimming near the shore in three feet of water. He described it in a social media post reproduced on the RiverheadLocal.com news site as "sick or something." Ten days later and three miles east, beachgoers on a Mattituck Sound beach recorded video of a large shark swimming in a few feet of water in the middle of the afternoon. I viewed the video, also on RiverheadLocal.com, and couldn't help think that there was something wrong with the shark to be almost up on the beach like that during the middle of the day.

Given the previous sightings not more than ten miles west of where Billy saw the shark behind his plug, it seemed possible that it could have been the same fish. I sent him links to the two news accounts, and he said the shark he saw looked similar to the one recorded in Mattituck. Given the rarity of shark sightings in these waters, it seemed like a reasonable explanation, until a couple of nights later when both he and his fishing partner had their eel leaders cut off after 100-yard screaming runs that were definitely too strong to be stripers or bluefish. His email report ended with "Might be time for you to make a sharking video hahaha." Even at this point, I discounted the notion of actually targeting sharks from a Sound beach. It seemed like a silly waste of time. I would need more nudging, and it came twelve days later.

The striper fishing had been pathetically slow for nearly a month, and non-existent before that. I had zero expectations of anything interrupting my retrieve as my wooden pencil popper danced its way toward me, closing to within sixty feet as the sun sank into the Sound to my left. I was fortunate not to slip off my rock when the plug was suddenly engulfed. The depths of the rod pumps told me *big*, as the fish rolled over with a broome-like tail in the air. I fought it aggressively through the boulders and was rather shocked to drag a 34-pound bass into the shallows. A nearby beachgoer snapped a picture, and the fish was sent on its way with the sun still partially visible above the horizon.

On a clear evening such as this, I feel that pencil poppers are effective up until around twenty-five minutes after sunset. Given the solid catch, I kept at it a few minutes beyond that. I had no intentions of fishing after dark. I was perched on a rock about forty feet from shore where it would be necessary to wade back starting in chest-high water. As this was August, I wore wading pants rather than waders. I would have to endure a brief cold-shock as I slid off the rock, but I would soon appreciate the lightweight pants in the warm and humid summer air as I walked back to my truck. I was sitting on the rock with my back to the water and about to slide in when I heard a massive *Whoosh* behind me. I turned around as fast as I could given my weed and barnacle-covered seat, and was not even surprised to see the largest boil I had ever witnessed outside of offshore fishing. The sound of it had already prepared me for the sight. I stood up as fast as I could, and pretty much froze as a large fin and tail broke the water's surface not fifty feet in front of me. My video camera was still on my head, but the creature slipped below the surface before it powered up. I lobbed a cast behind the residual boil, and then several more while fan-casting the area, but there was nothing but increasing darkness.

The forty feet that separated me from the safety of the beach now looked like the length of a football field as I surveyed the water darkened by the weedy bottom and diminished daylight. Growing up on Long Island's North Shore, I had almost zero exposure to sharks, and didn't know much about their behavior. I knew Long Island Sound shark attacks were very rare from having done some previous research motivated by the recent sightings.

I learned that there had been only one unprovoked attack on the Long Island side of the Sound. It occurred in 1865, but coincidently it had been at Greenport, just a couple of miles from where I was preparing to slip into the dark water with at least one large and feeding shark that had just been within fifty feet of me. I hesitated a moment thinking about the situation, but realized the longer I waited, the darker and higher the water would get. I kept the camera running, thinking somewhat jokingly that my widow could at least monetize my death on YouTube should I not make it to shore. After a relatively clean dismount into water up to my armpits, I put one foot in front of the other as quickly as I could on the irregular weed-covered bottom. It was a relief to hit thigh-deep water and the weed-free and light-colored stones that allowed me to see to the bottom. I would not look behind me until I was on the beach, afraid of what I might see. Given that more than two weeks had passed since Billy's first sighting, it was clear that there was more than one shark, and they were hanging around.

Several days later, I looked off the bluff in Greenport and saw large schools of bunker being annihilated by fish. None was closer than a half-mile from the beach, so I hooked up my boat and launched from the shore in East Marion. I am not a fan of snag and drop, but after numerous attempts of trying to interest fish with plugs and bucktails, I finally gave in and snagged and livelined a bunker to see what was pushing the fish. Amazingly, I had a lot of trouble getting any hits at all, despite using an 80-pound mono leader instead of wire. When a hookup finally came, it initially felt like I had snagged a slow-moving submarine. There was no give, just steady movement, which after about ten seconds accelerated into a drag scorching run that terminated in a cut leader about twenty seconds later. Given the events of the previous two weeks, I concluded it was a shark. While I was on the bunker schools, I saw my opportunity to secure some bait for a beach sharking attempt, so I kept a half-dozen and decided to freeze them not knowing when or if I'd actually try.

I did have one ocean beach sharking trip under my belt. It was several years prior when I was bored by the hot weather striper fishing and intrigued by the pictures of large sharks that were being beached at Smith Point Park, and along much of Long Island's South Shore. I probably never would have tried, but one evening I looked off the bluff in Wading River and saw perfect shark bait in the form of 1-pound bluefish chasing bait. I caught eight, put them on ice, and then spent more time than I should have researching shark rigs in work the next day. It turned out I already had everything I needed from a fishing trip to Key West where I had hoped to hook a shark from a rented kayak. I came up empty in my only attempt, but at least I still had the gear. The rig I settled on was pretty simple. There's at least a 5-foot leader of something like 80-pound-test leader material connected at the terminal end through a barrel swivel to a foot of single-strand wire with a large circle hook. There's a fishfinder and sinker on the leader material. At least that's what I came up with and tied when I got home from work. Because I had the permit to drive on the beach at Smith Point, this was to be a relatively lazy trip. It was only a half-hour from my house, and I'd drive a very short distance from the beach vehicle access point. I pre-tied only three rigs, guessing I might not need more than one, and knowing I could tie more while I was there. I needed a YouTube video to refresh my memory on the haywire twist connections on the ends of the single-strand wire.

I caught no sharks that night, but did beach a large butterfly ray with a 71-inch wingspan. These are considered gamefish in some states, and

I understood why given the great fight it gave with runs up and down the beach without ever digging into the bottom like typical stingrays do. With my two leftover rigs from that trip, and six bunker in the freezer, it didn't take much activation energy to put together what was needed for a shark attempt on the Sound beach. As I did on the ocean shark trip, I'd use my 11-foot jetty bass bucktailing rod. I built it in 1991 on a Lamiglas GSB1321M blank, which was quite a new offering back then, and a bit heavier with more stopping power than the ones made in later years. The reel would be the largest spinning reel I owned – a Penn 8500SSV spooled with 2-year-old 50-pound-test Spiderwire Stealth. I don't hesitate to use older braid as long as it's not worn.

My sharking attempt on a Long Island Sound beach was likely to be a one and done. It seemed like a stupid idea all along, but I just had to try, not wanting to look back years later and wonder if I could have hooked one to get a better idea of what kind and how large they actually were. The first decision I had to make was where to try. An obvious choice was to fish exactly where Billy and I had encountered sharks. The problem was that this area, like most of the North Fork of Long Island, is boulder strewn. If I managed to hook one it would obviously make a very long run, and it seemed inevitable my line would end up against a rock and I'd eventually get cut off. To have a chance at landing one, I should choose an obstruction-free beach such as McCabes or Southold Town Beach. I could even fish within casting distance of my truck there, although the thought of parking lot headlights and activity was very unattractive. However, at McCabes I could walk down the beach, be free from parking lot interference, and still be in an obstruction-free area with all of the room in the world to fight a large fish. In the end I decided to give myself the greatest odds of actually hooking a shark, and worry about the rocks later. I'd fish where I knew they had been.

Low slack was around sunset. You would think that there would be a better shot at these fish near high tide, but they were coming in close irrespective of the water level. I reasoned I'd be starting near slack, but then have hours of moving water in the darkness. Billy was there on my arrival, and I asked him if he wanted me to move well away of where he was bass fishing, but he said he was happy to have me fish close so he could see what happened. I generally don't fish cut bait, but I do understand the basics. You want to keep putting new meat in the water.

With six bunker that I could get two baits from each, I'd have 12 baits. I would keep track of the time and change to a new bait every twenty minutes. This would give me roughly four hours-worth of bait, which was plenty of time for this test. The only shark I'd probably see would be a dogfish.

I chose an easy perch to access and stand on, maybe thirty feet from shore, and in only thigh-deep water to start. The three-foot-high rock would give me a little extra height. The sun was half-way into the water with just a few thin clouds on the horizon. This gave off an orange glow as I waded out for my first cast. The water's surface was glassy in close, but turned to a deeper rippled blue at the end of lure casting range under the influence of an offshore breeze that was mostly blocked by the bluffs behind me. As my first cast of a big chunk hanging off a combined 6-foot leader and 3-ounce sinker was in the air, I felt like I could have thrown a pillow farther. "Is that gonna be far enough?" I asked Billy in a worried tone. "Are you kidding? I saw one chase something around that rock there," as he motioned to a rock sticking out of the water to my left but only twenty feet farther out than I was standing.

Apparently distance would be no problem. Lack of fish and boredom probably would be. I stayed on the rock I cast from and held the rod. I would not be using a sand spike. Should I actually get a hit, I wanted to be in the best possible position to deal with it, both for hooking and fighting the fish. Being a little bit farther out from the beach and standing higher than beach level would put me in a better position to fight a fish and keep the line high and hopefully away from rocks. I kept the reel's bail open, with my right hand holding the rod and my left hand holding the line. This way I could feel any pickup immediately. Should I hook a shark, I was equipped to capture the fight on video. My GoPro was accompanied by a very bright companion light. It could light up the beach like the headlights on a car. Its downside was short battery life at that intensity, maybe thirty minutes. Given the battery life limitation, and the fact that I didn't want a bright light shining on the water while I was trying to attract fish, I had a plan. When I felt a grab, I'd drop the line and turn the camera on with my left hand. Then I'd feel for the line and let it run through my hand as the fish moved with the bait. After maybe ten seconds, I'd engage the reel and crank. Should I connect solidly with the fish, I'd turn my light on.

As planned, I reeled in my first chunk and replaced it after twenty minutes. I repeated the procedure twenty minutes later, then twenty minutes after that. My fourth chunk was now in the water, and it was dark. Billy had managed just one schoolie bass in that time. I was bored, but determined to give it a fair shot on this beautiful evening and fish at least a couple of hours into the tide. Suddenly I felt a sharp tap on the line. I immediately let go of it, and to my amazement, it started going out. "Holy crap! I'm going to get a shot!" I said to no one, as Billy had waded down the shore and out of earshot. The line went off the spool fast for about five seconds, then stopped. I tried to feel for the bait but felt only slack. It's coming at me! I immediately engaged the reel and cranked as the line tightened quickly and the rod arched over as the reel surrendered a couple of yards of line against the tight drag. The "shark" then launched into the air with the unmistakable sound and landing of a large bluefish. I was disappointed that I didn't have a shark on, but understood fully that this was the next best thing, as fresh bluefish fillets would be far superior bait than the frozen bunker chunks that I had. In about a minute I had the long and skinny 12-pounder on the beach. I was rather amazed at my luck. No one had been catching any, and as it turned out, I wouldn't catch the next blue for another month. My plans had now changed. I had plenty of the best bait possible, and beautiful conditions. I would stay on the beach until the bluefish pieces ran out.

My next cast was with a bluefish fillet dripping with blood. A few minutes before I was to change it up, I had another grab, let it run, but missed it. I'll never know what that was, but I felt the water had life now. On both hits I was too focused on the fish to engage the camera and light. Billy had given up on the bass, so I was alone now.

Bluefish chunk number two hit the water. Boredom was now replaced with anticipation. Eight minutes later I felt a bump on the line, immediately dropping it to turn on my camera. Reaching down to find the line again wasn't necessary as it was clearly running through the guides fast. Feeling as though I might have come tight too quickly on the previous hit, I waited, recalling the last time I had shark fished in a boat eighteen years earlier and my friend Mike calmly said "Just let it run," prior to striking. That incident and the five-and-a-half-hour battle that followed was a chapter in my first book, *A Season on the Edge*. Having given the fish what I felt was plenty of time, I brought my rod tip high, engaged the bail, dropped my rod angle, and started reeling. I was not able to lift the rod again, as line screamed off for the next fourteen seconds, as measured on dark video because I was too shocked to turn on the light. The run ended abruptly, and I cranked for a long time to get the remains of my rig back. The loss was my fault. My original haywire twist was good, but the bluefish bent the wire where the hook was attached. I noticed this after unhooking the blue, and straightened the wire with my pliers. It looked OK, but it wasn't. That's where it broke. I was disappointed at my mistake, but I know what I don't know, and this kind of fishing was new to me. I did however actually hook a shark!

Now scared by the perceived fragility of the single strand wire, I tied a large circle hook on 60-pound test coated braided wire, like you would use for big bluefish. Anticipation was high now as my third bluefish chunk hit the water. By now I think the sharks had picked up on the scent I was dispersing in the water. I waited less than ten minutes for my next chance. I executed in the same fashion as the previous hit, right down to my failure to turn on the light. This run was shorter than the previous, as the shark easily bit through the coated wire. That was at least two blown chances. How many more could I get?

My feeling now went from anticipation to expectation as I felt as though I knew what would happen within a few minutes of my bait landing in the water. The hit came in about five minutes. I let it run, dropped the line, turned on the camera, waited a little longer, engaged the reel, cranked until the drag screamed, and for the first time – turned on the video light! I know enough to keep a good bend in a fishing rod when hooked up, but was unable to lift the rod past its low angle above the water. I could do nothing other than hold on as the fish surged with repeated bursts of speed separated by one-second pauses. Its power was far beyond any I had experienced with a striper against a drag that was set as tight as I dared without risking breakage of the 50-pound-test braid. Understanding the uniqueness of the situation, I began expressing my feelings out loud, knowing they were being recorded with the video. "Long Island Sound Shark!" was announced about thirty seconds into the run. Followed soon after by "I feel like I'm up against a rock, but I don't think it matters." It didn't matter because I thought I had about as much of a chance of stopping the fish as I would a moving boat, as I felt completely overpowered. About a minute into the run the distinct smell of burning drag washers permeated the air.

The hard running with the feeling of line rubbing and periodic short hangs lasted for five minutes, then I was just plain stuck. For most of that time I expected the line to part at any second, but somehow it didn't. I expressed frustration out loud that I felt like I had actually stopped the fish, but was unlikely to be able to pull it out of the rocks. The futility of it all hit home when I looked down and saw that my large spool was half empty. Still, I remained connected to the fish, and for the first time it felt like it was tired. I could do nothing but pull back slowly and firmly on the rod, then drop it down while putting a few turns of line on the reel. Although I was inexperienced doing this with a shark, I had done it successfully many times with large stripers. This works because many submerged boulders are covered heavily in weed growth, and it provides some protection for the line. If you can avoid putting a lot of pressure on the line, you can hear it squeak as it slides across the weeds. My problem was that I had to apply a lot of pressure to the shark, and just hope for the best. The other problem was that I was experiencing give and take, where I'd put some line on the reel, only to give most of it back on subsequent short runs. This meant the same sections of line were going back and forth over the rocks.

Starting six minutes into the fight, and lasting for the next six minutes, I made a long series of pulls followed by cranks to put line on the reel. The shark was tired, but its weight required a lot of pressure to move toward me even if it didn't actively resist. With progress being made, and two hangs cleared successfully. I began to feel some hope. The fish woke up with a brief burst of energy and a thrash on the surface close enough for me to say "Holy shit I see him!" For the first time I knew exactly where it was, and I was in trouble because between me and the fish was a rock sticking two feet out of the water. It would be very difficult for me to keep my line above that rock as the fish crossed behind it. With barnacles clearly visible on top, I was done if the line made contact with it.

Normally it would be hard for me to see exactly where my line was in relation to the rock, but given that I had already come into contact with so many submerged rocks, the line had numerous pieces of weed hanging off. Illuminated by my headlight, the clothesline of weed strands enabled me to see precisely how much clearance I had between my line and the rock. Considering how far I had managed to move the fish, I began thinking this rock could be my last big hurdle to landing it. That thought was interrupted by a short explosion of speed and lost line that that took me another minute to regain against a strengthening current. With total focus on clearing the last exposed rock, I hung again on a submerged boulder behind it, and this time I was stuck solid.

I was now faced with a choice. I was on a good perch with enough height to clear the problem rock, but the only way to potentially get out of the hang from my current position was to pull harder against almost certainly damaged line. My other option was to get off the perch and wade parallel to the shore to a point that I could change the angle on where the fish was hung, and possibly pull it out that way. This was fraught with complications and potential danger. "Could be a bad move!" were my last words before dismounting my rock into the dark water that clearly held a lot of sharks. I was wearing wading pants instead of waders, so I felt like I had just put two more pieces of meat in the water. At least if I had waders they would have prevented any scent from entering the water. I kept my rod high and waded deeper than my waist to get closer to and over the exposed rock that had threatened my line. Now I was much lower to the water, with a terrible angle on the hung shark. I scoured the water with my head light until it lit up another perch that was about thirty feet away in a direction parallel to the shore. It was a good feeling to get on top of that and get the lower half of my body out of the water, which in my mind now bordered on shark infested.

I was relieved to feel the shark still on the other end of the line as I applied pressure from my new position. I had a better angle slightly down current of the hang. I opened the bail and let the fish move off on its own, hoping it would move with the current and away from the hang. It worked! In a few pulls I was free again, and seconds later had a clear view of the shark's dorsal fin. This was a milestone, as I wanted video proof that I definitely had a shark on, and not something like a big ray. With a clear view of first the dorsal, then the entire shark, I worked it close to my perch so that I could visually steer it by any other submerged rocks. Jumping back into the waist deep water with it just beyond my rod tip was unnerving, but I was now focused more on winning the battle than on worrying about it attacking me. Seconds later it swam straight at me twice to my pleading "Don't come near me!" Now scared of its behavior while I was at its mercy and still more than thirty feet from shore, I made a very deliberate move toward the beach. With my feet moving and my rod held out away from me, I dragged the shark to the side and behind me until I was in less than two feet of water, thus eliminating any reasonable chance of being bit. From my safer position, I kept the pressure on and inched its massive weight shallower until it finally bottomed out. I did it!

Trying to move the big shark through the shallows.

I was not sure, but I guessed correctly that this was a Brown Shark, which is one of several "Prohibited" sharks that should not be removed from the water. That would not be a problem, as there was no reason to move it any farther. I was happy that it was still partially submerged. I had a still camera on me, but I was not overly concerned about still photos, knowing that I had it all on video. I was happy to see that the circle hook worked exactly as it was designed to, and was embedded in the corner of the shark's mouth. I am not at all embarrassed to say that I was afraid of the shark. I had heard too many stories of sharks that were thought to be dead suddenly exploding into a burst of violence. I did not want to lift the shark's head to get at the hook, nor did I want to spend time with my hand close as I attempted to work it out of its jaw. I opted instead to cut the wire leader as close to the shark's mouth as I dared.

As I was about to do that, I heard the crunching of beach stones as someone approached. It was a bait fisherman who had been quite a distance down the beach and was drawn to all of the commotion of my bright light. "Grande!" was really the only word I understood from him, but I handed him the camera and motioned for him to take some shots while I dealt with the fish. He did a great job and I was happy to find some nice pictures on the camera when I got home.

I was nervous about releasing the fish, which was still quite lively. With a hand on its dorsal, I carefully turned it around and pointed it away from the shore. I moved it into slightly deeper water while holding the dorsal fin, feeling that this gave me a little control over it turning its head to bite me. Once I was in more than two feet of water, I let go and was relieved to see it swimming out in "S" shaped sweeps. I followed it out a little, as I would with a released bass, but not too far as I knew the shark could turn around and come back at me. While still a surf rod's length away, my light quit and left me momentarily in total darkness until I could turn on the small light around my neck. I quickly looked around with it, but the shark was thankfully gone.

This was a newsworthy catch, and given the recent sightings and local interest, I sent a couple of the still pictures off to the local community paper, and to the late Fred Golofaro at *The Fisherman*. The story eventually made it to *News12*, which gave it airtime on both sides of the Sound for a couple of days. Before I let anyone other than friends in on the catch, I thought carefully about how I would explain it. I found the NYS regulations concerning shore fishing for sharks to be murky at best. The regulations at the time said it was "Illegal to take or possess prohibited shark species." The regulations went on to say "Do not fish for prohibited sharks." Prohibited sharks included Brown (Sandbar), Dusky, and Sand Tiger. The regulations continued with "These three species are primarily the only species of large shark anglers will encounter from shore." So, while they explicitly say it's illegal to keep these sharks, they did not say explicitly that it was illegal to shark fish from the shore. I already knew that shore sharking wasn't illegal, because as mentioned earlier, shark fishing from Long Island ocean beaches in the summer had become very popular and was catered to by numerous tackle shops. Shore sharking was done in the open with pictures and video posted frequently to social media with no apparent repercussions from the New York State Department of Environmental Conservation.

One of the reasons it was not illegal was that other non-prohibited species of sharks, such as Threshers and Blacktips, were also caught from Long Island beaches. In fact, in the weeks leading up to my catch, there were several news stories about a large number of Blacktip sharks in Long Island waters. When sharks were suddenly in Sound waters where I wouldn't expect them, I thought maybe these were the Blacktips, which commonly feed close to shore. As for the statement "Do not fish for prohibited sharks.", I don't think the angler has much say in what takes their bait. Taking all of this into account, I felt comfortable that I hadn't broken any laws by throwing meat chunks into the Sound on gear that might handle a shark. When asked however, I decided it was best to distort my reasons for soaking cut bait on the beach that night. I was not interested in initiating a directed fishery for sharks on the otherwise quiet North Fork beaches. It was now clear that there were a lot of sharks, and from my brief test, they were pretty easy to hook up. If somebody else found them during what I now think of as the *summer of sharks*, fine, but I wasn't going to be the one to let the cat out of the bag. It was more sensible and more believable to say I caught it accidently while fishing for bluefish, and so I did.

A sight I never thought I'd see on a Long Island Sound beach.

CHAPTER 17
SEA BASS JIGGING

I watched the fishfinder as my boat skimmed across the glass-calm surface of Long Island Sound on a cool fall morning. The bottom 70 feet below rose gradually until peaking at 58 feet, before dropping a little more abruptly to 65 feet, where I pulled the throttle back to neutral and turned the boat broadside into the first breaths of the ebb tide. I stopped any residual forward motion by putting the engine briefly into reverse, stopping the boat dead at the top of the drift.

The 6-foot medium spinning rod was ready to go with a plain 1-ounce olive bucktail. I dropped it to the bottom while staring intensely at the line, which contrasted well against the dark-green water. At the first sight of a tick in the line followed by slack, I snapped the rod skyward and then watched the line for the next bottom collision that would be my signal to snap the rod skyward again. On the next repetition, the jig stopped short on the fall, initiating my hook-setting reflex. The rod arched over with the drag giving line to whatever grabbed my jig on its descent. The fish took a little line and put up good resistance all the way to the boat. The 4-pound black sea bass was a respectable catch, but would make an even more noteworthy dinner.

If you want to catch a lot of sea bass, put squid or clam on a hook and send it to the bottom with a sinker. In the many areas in the Northeast that are nearly infested with these fish, you'll catch plenty. Most will be well short of whatever the legal limit is, and very few will exceed the 18-inch-plus fish that I target. If you want to catch those, then leave the

A 1-ounce bucktail without a trailer pulled this sea bass from 60 feet of water in Long Island Sound.

bait in the boat, and fish either plain bucktails or diamond jigs.

If you're a regular follower of my fluke fishing videos, you know I generally hate sea bass when they interfere with our fluke fishing and devour our pricey Gulp grubs. While I'll often curse them while fluke fishing, next to cod, I think they're the best eating fish in Northeast inshore waters. On top of that they grow to respectable size, put up a great fight on relatively light tackle, and the larger ones hit artificials aggressively. That last part is the key, because it allows you to cull the big hard-fighting ones with the nice fillets from the seemingly endless number of small sea bass that blanket the bottom in many areas of good structure.

If conditions permit, I don't know of a more effective or fun way to catch big sea bass than the bucktail jigging described above. The use of 10-pound-test braided line is a key to this fishing. Not only should the line be no thicker than 10-pound-test braid, it needs to be a color that stands out against the water, because you absolutely must see it clearly to know when the jig hits the bottom and needs to be snapped skyward. Many anglers choose bright yellow line for this fishing. I use Berkley X9 Crystal, which appears white out of the water and shows up well.

If you've read my *Fishing the Bucktail* book, you might recall that I gave John Paduano and his Premium bucktails a couple of pages of ink there to mention snap jigging, a technique that he has championed in the

Northeast for quite some time. The idea is that the whip, or *snap*, of the rod when the jig hits the bottom causes the bucktail to dart away quickly, but for a limited distance. This simulates a baitfish trying to flee, forcing the fish to have to make a very hasty decision as to whether or not to hit. The simulated fleeing prey often triggers a fish to chase and grab the perceived meal before it escapes. Although John often demonstrates or describes this technique in the context of casting and retrieving in depths less than 45 feet, the same principles apply in deeper water. However, it can be very challenging to keep a 1-ounce jig near the bottom while casting and retrieving in 65 feet of water with substantial current. It's much easier to do by dropping the jig straight down as described in the opening paragraph. As the drift proceeds, you may need to periodically let out additional line to stay near the bottom, similar to fluke jigging. If the current conditions don't allow you to stay down with the ideal 1-ounce weight, you can go heavier to a 1.5, or even a 2-ounce jig. Beyond that, you're probably better off with a diamond jig. Yo-yoing a diamond jig will be almost as much fun and productive, and we'll get to that in a bit.

Depth is not what determines how much weight you need to stay down. It's not even the current speed. Rather it's the difference between the current speed near the bottom and the current speed higher in the water column, all of the way to the surface. You can fish in 100 feet of water with less than an ounce if the current speed is uniform throughout

If the current becomes too strong for bucktailing sea bass, a diamond jig will often get the job done.

the water column. When the water is moving, this is rarely the case. Add even a light breeze to the setting, and you're almost assured that the boat will be drifting at a different speed than the bottom current. The way to keep your lightweight jig near the bottom in the typical scenario where the boat moves at a different speed than the bottom water is to minimize the drag on your line. Not to confuse this with the mechanical drag on your reel, I'm referring to how much your line resists being dragged through the water. The two main variables that effect line drag are diameter and smoothness.

Not all 10-pound-test braids are the same. Most quality braided lines will have the line diameter printed on the spool and/or packaging. You can often find this information online. Take note of it and choose one of the lower diameter brands. That takes care of one variable. You can learn something about the smoothness of a line by considering the strand count where you'll see something like "8-strand" or "4-strand." The word "carrier" might be used in place of "strand." This refers to the number of strands woven together to make the line. The greater the strand count, the smoother the line, and therefore the less drag in the water. At the time of this writing, all of my jigging lines were at least 8-strand, usually Berkley X9 or Daiwa J-Braid 8.

Rod choice is almost as important as line choice. Whether casting and retrieving, or dropping straight to the bottom, snap jigging is difficult to do with a rod longer than about 6.5 feet. The rod should have moderate action so that it loads up and springs the jig forward or up when you whip it. There are custom rod builders who make rods specifically for this fishing. Matt at Eastern Rod Works is one. I've known Matt since he worked at Wading River Bait and Tackle and Rocky Point Fishing Stop when I lived in that area. He has been trained by the best and does a great job. J&H Tackle in Oakdale has a spinning version of the Dark Matter Skinner Jig and Bounce rod that became so popular for fluke jigging and blackfish. That rod is ideal for the deeper vertical snap jigging described above. At the time of this writing, I was working through prototypes for a lighter version. That rod will be patterned after a modified old Abu Garcia rod that appears in some of my videos. It might be available by the time you're reading this. This fishing can be tiring, so you want to keep the rod and reel weight down. A 2000- to 3000-size reel is appropriate.

Bucktails for this fishing will usually not have trailers of any kind, should look realistic, and should sink easily with minimum weight. Densely tied bucktails with lots of hair, feathers, and smiling bill heads are the wrong bucktails for this because they're designed to swim above shallow structure, rather than get to the bottom fast. Ball-head jigs are the most commonly used. I use S&S Gulf Series bucktails. Paduano's Premium bucktails are another excellent choice. Both of these bucktails have high-quality hooks that penetrate well and are strong enough to handle big fish. That's important because the snap jigging technique is deadly on big stripers and other gamefish. I doubt I've ever bucktailed sea bass without catching some stripers and/or bluefish as bycatch. You want that bucktail to look and fall naturally, so choice of leader thickness is a consideration. I use a 3-foot leader of 30-pound-test Fluorocarbon because it has a minimal effect on the presentation while giving me some abrasion resistance for bottom structure and bluefish.

Black sea bass are now found just about everywhere there's structure in the Northeast. I target them in the eastern Long Island Sound rips east of Mattituck. Current speeds peak at over three knots in some of the best areas, and given that the fish are often concentrated on specific parts of the irregular bottom structure, efficient fishing calls for short drifts. I typically do not try to catch more than one sea bass per drift there. The waters on both sides of Montauk Point and east to Block Island are ideal for this type of sea bass fishing, and generally allow for longer drifts. As with fluke drifting, trolling motors can be phenomenal tools for this kind of fishing because they can be used to negate the effect of wind, allowing one to keep the line vertical with minimal weight while drifting. When fishing significant current, anchoring does not work well for this fishing because the current will sweep the jig away from the stationary craft.

Sometimes the wind and current are such that it's impossible to stay down and make a good presentation with a small bucktail. That's when I'll break out the diamond jigs to keep catching. The concept is similar in that you'll want to touch the bottom and sweep upward, but the jigs will typically range between 3 and 5 ounces. With that much weight, there's no reason to not add a teaser ahead of the jig. A plain feather teaser works well at times, or you might go with a soft plastic or Gulp grub in the 4- to 6-inch range on a 5/0 Gamakatsu Baitholder hook. In addition to chrome jigs, I like to have glow and/or black with me, given the diamond jig color tests described in the weakfish chapter.

Back in the 70's and 80's, black sea bass were a novelty in many of the Northeast waters where they are plentiful now. The smaller ones can be a nuisance as they interfere with efforts to catch other species such as fluke, but the larger ones are as enjoyable on the end of the rod as they are on the dinner table. Bucktails and diamond jigs can put those big ones in your cooler, all while keeping your boat clean of the stench of clams and squid.

Katie and a big sea bass that hit a bucktail.

CHAPTER 18
PORGY JIGGING

If porgies grew to 10 or 15 pounds, they would probably be the most sought-after fish in Northeast waters. They fight very hard for their size, and are delicious on the dinner table. One of the first boat trips I make each season is for jumbo porgies in the Peconic Bay system. Two- to three-pound *scup*, as they're also known, are common there in early to mid-May. While most anglers target them there with standard hook and sinker rigs and unnecessarily heavy gear, I jig them on light tackle and have a ball. The same technique works equally well in Long Island Sound and many other areas during the rest of the season.

The S&S Skinner blackfish/porgy jigs that I wrote about in the blackfish chapter were born from an email I sent to Stanley at S&S asking for a jig that had a hook small enough to catch porgies, but strong enough to handle big blackfish. The jig he came up with initially was a winner, but he has since improved on it and created a custom mold. Tipped with a small piece of squid, a jig of 1 ounce or less fished on a light spinning rod with 10-pound-test braid is all you need to have lots of fun and plenty of fish in the cooler. If you have blackfish jigging gear, then you're already set for porgies, provided your jigs have the appropriate size hooks.

Big Peconic porgies show up in the first days of May and can be caught in good numbers and size for most of the month. I find the best time to go is the first half of the month, before big bluefish invade the bay. While you can find them throughout the bay system from eastern

Shelter Island Sound to west of Robbins Island, the most heavily fished area is a little west of Jessup's Neck. This is no secret, as it's not unusual to see fifty plus boats there, including party boats from Connecticut and Montauk, and others docked locally specifically for the porgy run.

Big porgies are a lot of fun on light tackle and jigs.

While I typically don't chum for porgies in Long Island Sound, I always do when I fish Jessup's. My feeling is that so many other boats chum there, that if I don't, the porgies will just go to where the chum is. Frozen clam chum is priced reasonably, and a block will last around 45 minutes. I always use squid that I buy from local tackle shops. The squid that I get from WEGO Bait and Tackle in Southold is caught locally, and even when purchased frozen, is in great condition. These are large squid that will produce thick strips that I thread on the jig hook. I don't leave much of the strip hanging off the back, because I want the porgies to grab the part of the squid strip with the hook in it. Many anglers use clams, but I've found that squid works at least as well, stays on the hook better, and costs less. One large squid will sometimes be all I need for a couple of hours of non-stop action. An advantage of fishing with jigs is that they tend to cull the larger porgies from the mixed sizes that are usually under the boat.

The Jessup's porgy area is large. I start by motoring slowly around contour lines in about 35 feet of water while watching the fishfinder for life. When I see fish near the bottom, I shut down and drift. When I start catching sizeable porgies, which has never taken more than a couple of minutes, I anchor and put the chum out. Once the chum goes down the porgies find it very quickly. At this point the bites should be nearly instantaneous when your jig hits the bottom. If the chum has been down for 45 minutes or longer and the bite begins to slow and/or you notice sea robins mixing in, then it's time to make sure you still have chum left. This approach has never failed me. I've caught well on both tides at Jessup's, but prefer the incoming because the current is a little weaker. The area that I fish experiences an eddy where the water is almost always flowing to the east, but the flow is stronger on outgoing current.

A big Peconic porgy.

It's always good to have a backup plan when fishing, and you should have one when targeting porgies at Jessup's in May, but not for the usual reason that you might expect. Maybe I've just hit it right, or maybe it's because I start these trips in the early morning, but so far I've caught all of the porgies I've wanted in less than two hours. The bag limit has been overly generous at times, allowing an angler to keep as many as 30 porgies. I don't need all of that meat, I certainly don't want to clean that many, and I'm cognizant of the fact that these fish are on their spawning grounds. At most I'll keep a dozen nice ones and release at least an equal number. Fortunately the bay abounds with options in May, including bass and blues less than two miles to the east at Buoy 17, weakfish in Noyack Bay, and Fluke at Greenlawns and Greenport. Have some 2- to 4-ounce diamond jigs for Jessup's and Noyack Bay, and be sure to have spares because the bluefish can cut them off. All of this is within about five miles of a New York State boat ramp in Southold that opened in 2021. While I'm not typically in the habit of mentioning access points, it's a big bay system with many places to fish for multiple species, so I don't see much harm in passing this on to readers of this book.

I fish the same way for porgies in Long Island Sound, but typically don't chum because it attracts too many small sea bass and tiny porgies. I usually target them within a couple of hundred yards from shore in 20- to 30-feet of water. Areas with boulders are good, but you don't need to be right next to a rock to catch, as is usually the case with blackfish. This fishing gets going around the time Peconic Bay slows down in late May, and stays strong into the fall.

Porgy numbers seem limitless at times, but keep in mind that this is never the case with any fish. Besides, no one I know wants to fillet a few dozen porgies. Even if you just bring a single pack of frozen squid with you and a few ¾-to 1 ½-ounce jigs with the right-size hooks, you'll have kept the porgy option open in many Northeast waters. Porgies will never be a glamour fish, but they're a lot of fun on light tackle, great eating, and can be a nice addition to any multi-species trip.

Katie and friends had a good time on the porgy grounds.

CHAPTER 19
THE CREW

The most unexpected consequence of moving to Greenport in early 2017 was that the majority of my fluke fishing would shift to the hallowed grounds between Montauk and Block Island. I actually thought that by moving to the North Fork, I was moving farther from the ocean because I'd have to drive around from the North Fork to get to the South Shore. Indeed, my ocean surf fishing spots were now farther away. Even if it had occurred to me that Montauk was only 30 miles from Greenport over water, having never owned anything more capable than a 16-ft tin boat put the thought of running out of Greenport to boat fish at Montauk well out of the range of possibilities. That all changed thanks to a chance encounter at the New England Saltwater Fishing Show in Providence Rhode Island, two months after moving *out east*. As significant as that encounter became, the only thing I remember of it was that the person across the table from me was expressing doubt that light tackle fluke bucktailing would work well when he fished "70 feet of water behind Claudio's." That's a famous and historic restaurant on the water in downtown Greenport, and an equally well-known landmark for early season fluke anglers. The conversation was one of hundreds I had across my table over the course of the three-day show, that included me giving a seminar each day, and was soon forgotten until I received a Facebook message from the angler several days later.

"John, I'm the Greenport guy you met in Rhode Island last week. First, your book is great - read it cover to cover. Second, when I told my friends I met you and that you were moving to Greenport, I caught a lot of flak for not inviting

you to fish with us. Consider this an open invitation. I own a 1-year-old 25 Cobia that we frequently take to Montauk for some giant fluke (not to mention our secret Peconic Bay spots)... Anyway, you're always welcome to fish with us. I'm sure you hear this all the time and understand if you prefer to do your own thing but know you have this open invite."

He was correct that I was frequently offered trips on other people's boats. To this point every single offer had been declined. The main reason I turned everyone down was that I was just too busy. I will never understand how I managed to work fulltime in my day-job that demanded innovative and near perfect software development, while at the same time fishing a lot and pulling off the whole fishing-related business. There was just no free time to head out with someone else. My knee-jerk response to the offer to fish was to start typing the usual "I really appreciate the offer to fish on your boat, but between my day-job, family responsibilities, and my own fishing-related activities..." as I would try to gracefully extricate myself from whatever kind offer was coming my way so I could protect the flexibility needed to deal with all of life's demands. Before completing my response, I paused a moment. This guy's boat was docked less than a mile from my new home. The actual fishing grounds were less than a mile from there. It's possible that the downright excitement of having just moved to a harbor town on the edge of awesome fishing grounds clouded my judgement, but I sat back from the keyboard and began seriously considering the offer.

Who was this person? I recalled having a conversation with someone about fishing in front of Claudio's, but that was it. This wasn't necessarily a bad thing, because the vast majority of people I meet at the fishing shows are very nice people. If the guy had been a jerk, that probably would have stuck in my mind. There have been some very memorable table encounters. Like the guy who looked at me in amazement and said "I thought you died!" Or another that introduced me to someone else while explaining that "A lot of people hate this guy but he's a great fisherman." A lot of people hate me? What did I do? This is why I stay off of social media as much as possible. Most memorable in a way that I'll never forget was a father in tears explaining how his teenage son basically hadn't left his bedroom in two years, until he somehow found and started following my YouTube videos. "Dad, I'd like to go fishing," was the kid's first step out of his isolation. Before long, father and son were enjoying fishing trips together, and eventually the boy recovered. The father was so thankful for me, as he saw it, saving his son. That encounter made up for learning that lots of people hate me.

By default, the offer to fish my new very local waters was coming from someone who was OK. It did not escape me that I might actually learn something, given that I had never fluke fished these waters before. This was only a minor consideration though, because I had gone through my fishing life figuring out pretty much everything on my own. I was not used to, nor would I seek out, information from others. This came partially from reclusive surfcasting. My feeling was that if I had any kind of a fishing network from which I received anything more than seasonal progression information, then I'd be obligated to reciprocate. Stated more bluntly, if someone told me about a good fishing spot, I'd be obligated to share with that person anything I found. As mostly a loner surfcaster, this just didn't work for me. I'd rather do the analysis and work, and then keep my findings and spots to myself. Although I consider most fluke fishing much less secretive, the YouTube-related business aspect of my fishing was now something I considered a constraint on information sharing. If someone showed me a good under-the-radar fishing spot, and there were recognizable landmarks, then I'd feel as though I couldn't post video from there because it wasn't mine to risk burning. If I found something on my own, and I perceived that I wouldn't impact others by publishing video from that spot, then it would be fair game. Somewhat hesitantly, I tapped on the backspace key on my keyboard, erasing my declination of the offer to fish on the stranger's boat, replacing it with "Thanks. Yep. I get these offers frequently from Nantucket to Texas. Have declined every one so far, until now. Let me know when you're doing a local fluke trip. I'll bring the Gulp!"

When someone asked me what I'd miss most about moving from my previous home in Wading River, I answered "My mechanic." Trustworthy mechanics are hard to come by, and I had one at D&S automotive in Wading River. The shop was a little more than a mile from where I lived, which could be walked in a pinch. The owner, Perry, was an avid fisherman, and I would sometimes give talks at his North Brookhaven Sportfishing Club. I always knew he'd do a good job and not rip me off. I had no idea where to get my Jeep worked on in Greenport. I chose the closest garage, only ½-mile from my new home, but run by a guy who according to two Yelp reviews was "loud and larger than life." Still, I had to start somewhere, and I decided I'd feel out the place by letting him do an oil change on my wife's car before allowing him to touch the Jeep. I received a call from the shop on a Saturday morning indicating that the car was done, so I walked into town to pick it up. I was still nervous about the shop's owner, but before I could get to him, I was greeted by one of two guys hanging out at the garage drinking coffee. "John Skinner!" exclaimed one of them, who detected immediately that I had no idea who he was. "It's John Halkias, we've been corresponding on Facebook and you said you'd come fishing with us."

My failure to recognize him, and almost everyone else I've ever met, is worthy of some ink because it impacts most of my in-person interactions. I have a mild form of a condition called *face-blindness*. I first realized there was something wrong with me the summer after my freshman year of college. I was at a club in Hampton Bays with a friend and we encountered three girls that we had both gone to high school with. I hadn't just gone to school with them, I had ridden the school bus with them for four years. Given that the school was 20 miles from my home, it was a long bus ride and I probably spent close to two hours per school day in the presence of these girls. On top of that I went to grammar school with two of them, so I knew those two for roughly 12 years. As the five of us met and exchanged greetings, it was very obvious that they knew me. Like out of a scene from an episode of *Seinfeld*, I hung in with the conversation while pretending as best I could that I knew them, but finally gave up. "I'm sorry, but I don't remember who you are." My interpretation of the collective reaction from them was something like "What the hell is wrong with you?" They must have thought that I'd been brain damaged somehow during the year since they had last seen me. When the three girls together with my friend told me who they were, I felt like an absolute idiot.

When decades later I heard the term *face blindness* and looked up the symptoms, I felt a sense of relief. Among other things, it explained my difficulty in following some TV shows because I had trouble differentiating the characters. When my face blindness research explained that people with this condition develop compensation strategies to help identify individuals, I understood why I would as a matter of habit associate different surfcasters I'd meet with their vehicle or even their surf rod. For example, in my first several meetings of a local surfcaster in Baiting Hollow, I took note that he had an S-Glass rod with a nice spiral wrap and a Penn 5500. In time I could eventually recognize him on the beach without studying the rod, but all bets were off if I met him out of the beach context, such as in the grocery store.

I explain all of this because now that I've become somewhat of a public figure in fishing, the problem goes beyond forgetting a few school girls. If I meet you at a fishing show, and you come back to my table ten minutes later, I'll only recognize that I've met you previously if you're wearing or carrying something noteworthy. I know I've insulted people I've had long conversations with because I failed to recognize them even a short time later. It's not intentional. It's just that many humans look alike to me.

Halkias didn't seem put off that I didn't recognize him, and was quick to introduce me to his dentist-friend, John Keriazes, AKA *Doc*. He immediately yelled to the shop owner, George, "This is Skinner – the guy we were just telling you about!" I very much appreciated the potential to get in the good graces of the local mechanic. Doc explained to me that he sometimes saw my boat off Buoy 5, where we both fluke fished in the Sound. The conversation somehow changed to blackfishing local wrecks, and how he'd watch Nick Karas leave the inlet and note his direction to get some hint as to where the *Karas Wreck* was. Nick Karas was a fishing journalist for many years, and would write about tremendous catches on his secret wreck a couple of times each season. I had Doc scrambling for a pen and paper when I rattled off from memory the precise pair of 6-digit coordinates of that wreck that I had fished numerous times, occasionally close enough to Karas' boat to hold a conversation. Doc felt like he was in the presence of some fishing savant at that point, with me pulling those numbers out of my brain at the mere mention of the wreck. The truth is, those were the only coordinates I had ever memorized. The wreck was that good.

Our trip was planned for a couple of days after the opening day of fluke season, which that year fell on Wednesday, May 17th. Even with my inexperience fishing those waters, I understood that the mid-May opening was brutally late for the Peconic Bay system, where fluke show up in late April. Upon my mention that I'd sneak out in my boat opening day for a couple of hours before work, John offered some help. "Do you need any spot recommendations or do you want to prospect without prejudice to what I think?" Given my desire to get to my office, almost an hour from my new home, without anyone noticing that I was late, I was happy for a potential shortcut to a quick opening day limit. "I'm definitely open to spot recommendations for Wednesday, keeping in mind I want to stay within a couple of miles of Gull Pond because I'll probably fish a couple of hours and then go to work," I responded. John gave me three areas to try. Two would have been obvious, Claudio's and the oyster factory, because they were well-known and heavily-fished. The third spot was a little away from the rest.

"The Crew" on their 25-ft Cobia.

The sun rose at 5:30 a.m. on opening day, and I launched early enough to see it climb out of the water behind the Long Beach Bar Lighthouse, known locally as *Bug Light*. High tide was two hours earlier, so I'd have plenty of ebb current to start and nearly 4 hours to fish before slack tide. Not being a fan of fishing in crowds, I decided to start in the less pressured spot John gave me. I was confused by what I found when I shut the boat down to fish. "This sucks. There's no drift," was my initial reaction as I dropped my 3-ounce bucktail to the bottom and began jigging while noting a drift speed on my GPS between 0 and 0.3 mph. It would take the rest of the trip to realize it, but I was getting my introduction to fact that the strong currents and winding irregular shorelines of Shelter Island Sound produced eddys and dead spots. This is true of many waters with current and winding shores. In retrospect, I had overshot where John told me to go, and I landed on a dead spot. I stayed only a couple of minutes before moving on.

My next stop was behind Claudio's where I joined many more boats than I was used to fishing around. Still, I was excited to fish there because I wanted to see what the big attraction was. The only thing big there were the bluefish that put up a great fight but wrecked my rigs. Because I had to pass by the first spot to get to the oyster factory, I decided to give it another try, noting that two other boats were now in the general area, but a little east of where I tried initially. I planned to take one drift there, which would put me a little closer to the next spot.

It was evident immediately that there was plenty of current and a good drift. I had no idea where to start, so I studied my plotter and chose a contour line in around 50 feet of water. It produced only sea robins on the first drift, which was in the perfect 1- to 1.2-mph range. Given such a nice drift, I decided to move in a little and try again, this time focusing on a contour line in roughly 40 feet of water. I was only about a minute into that drift when my jigging was interrupted by the feeling of weight. When I swung the rod skyward, it barely budged. My first keeper in my new waters was a little over 6 pounds. I took a GPS mark on that and repeated the drift a few more times, adding a pair of four-pounders for an early 3-fish limit. I made it to my office by 10 a.m. without anyone imagining I had already accomplished a successful boat fishing trip 40 miles east. John's spot advice was dead-on and made it possible.

Two days after my successful opening day solo trip, I met John and Doc at the Cobia docked in Sterling Harbor. They introduced me to John's boat partner, John Sweeney, who Halkias described in a serious tone as one of Connecticut's best-known slumlords. In googling *Sweeney slumlord Connecticut*, when I arrived home, I learned that this was unlikely to be true. It wouldn't take long to realize that these guys were skilled at busting on each other, and it was only a matter of time before I got sucked in. In addition to food and soft drinks being loaded onto the boat, I spotted the squid and spearing. I was actually pleased to see this because I had no intention of using the stuff, but was anxious to out-fish it with bucktails and Gulp. As the four Johns headed out the harbor it was agreed that Sweeney and I would fish jigs and Gulp, while the others fished bait. Our modest results that day favored bucktails and Gulp heavily enough that I don't recall anyone bringing squid and spearing for fluke after that.

Something that impressed me about the crew was that we got a fishing report phone call while we were on the water, and it was from on-duty local law enforcement. It was regarding weakfish at Jessup's. We were off the South Fork at that time, and not in a position to get there. The same officer in his marked vehicle met us at the dock to chat when we returned. It demonstrated that at least someone on the crew was fairly well-connected locally. A week or so later we did another bay trip in which we had solid fishing on the South Fork side of the bay. It was there that I met a mild-mannered former French perfume executive in an awesome looking center console aluminum boat. It wasn't long before I became a regular on Rick Kohut's *Blu-J*, a 32-foot custom Metal Shark Fearless. This unique fishing machine absolutely ate up the slop around Montauk Point. This all laid the groundwork for what would become great friendships and phenomenal access to the ocean fluke fishery between Montauk and Block Island.

"Doc", Halkias, myself, and Sweeney with entries in a North Fork fluke tournament.

CHAPTER 20
OCEAN FLUKE

That won't work in water deeper than 40 feet. That statement, or some variation of it, was something I heard repeatedly when I first started promoting the advantages of light tackle fluke jigging with bucktails and Gulp, as opposed to the traditional approach of dragging natural baits. Starting in May of 2010, I began posting YouTube videos of my kids and I bucktailing fluke in Long Island Sound. No one could argue with how well the bucktail and Gulp technique worked, because I had video evidence, but all of the fishing was in a maximum of about 40 feet of water. At my first opportunity, I began fishing the ocean south of Shinnecock Inlet by any means possible, including my kayak, friends' boats, and even a rare party boat trip. The bulk of this fishing took place in 70-85 feet of water, especially around the Shinnecock reef. As I expected, bucktails and Gulp rigs worked just as well there as they did in the shallower Sound waters. The only change was in the use of heavier 2- to 4-ounce bucktails, as opposed to the ½- to 1 ½-ounce jigs I used in the Sound and shallow South Shore bays.

I knew I was going to like John Halkias when he told me to meet him at his boat at 4:30 a.m. for a fluke trip to Montauk's South Side. I understood that anyone leaving the dock at that hour for fluke was pretty serious. Our plan was to fish the Frisbees area in about 70 feet of water. We arrived near slack low water, and the fishing was slow for the first hour or so. Once the flood current started pushing toward the Lighthouse with the help of a light southwest wind, the bite lit up. I used the same rapid jigging presentation that I used everywhere else, and the fish pounded my rig. At some point when I stuck a third consecutive fish, I heard Halkias say "I'm not liking you anymore John." He was smart enough to watch what I was doing and made some adjustments to his jigging. It paid off for him with the best fish of the trip, an 8.9-pounder. My best were 7 and 8.2 pounds. We also had some smaller *Montauk keepers*, meaning 4- to 5-pounders, and left the fish biting as we already had a limit on ice and the wind started picking up.

John Halkias with a fluke caught on my first trip with him to Montauk.

As we were cleaning up, he invited me for a trip the following weekend. "We're going to fish Cartwright. Bucktails won't work out there. We'll have to fish bait on long leaders." When I finished laughing, I accepted his invitation and told him I wouldn't be needing any bait, as I was sure bucktails would work fine. The bucktails worked better than fine, and years later Halkias is now a top charter captain who specializes in bucktailing doormat Montauk fluke, many of which are caught at Cartwright.

His trepidation concerning the feasibility of light tackle fluke bucktailing there was well-founded. The water depth is in the 80- to 100-foot range with a mostly rocky bottom washed by significant current. It's among the most challenging settings to jig effectively for doormat fluke with relatively light gear. In the same way that the spook plug chapter could be seen as an additional chapter to my *Striper Pursuit* book, this could be considered a new chapter in my *Fishing for Summer Flounder* book. While what I write here applies to the many similar environments in the

Northeast, the focus will be on Montauk. I'll start with the basics for the sake of completeness and the benefit of those not familiar with my *Fishing for Summer Flounder* book or my videos.

I tie the same simple rig that I use for all of my fluke fishing. I use 30-pound-test leader material with a surgeon's loop at the bottom to connect the jig, and a dropper loop a foot above that to connect a teaser. My preferred teaser is a silicone skirt Tsunami Glass Minnow, but there are many fine fluke teasers on the market. A plain Gamakatsu 5/0 Baitholder hook with a Gulp Grub is sometimes as effective as anything else, and has the advantage of minimal drag in the water. I leave at least two feet of leader above the dropper loop to facilitate swinging fish over the side. I connect all of my leaders to the main line by going through a small high quality barrel swivel. Both my jig and teaser are tipped with 5- or 6-inch Gulp Grubs. If I had to choose one color, it would be glow white. Other very good Gulp colors are Pink Shine, Blue Fuze, and Salmon Red.

The objective is to fish with as light a jig weight as possible without *scoping out*. You're scoping out when you have to keep letting out line to stay near the bottom. The most common way to counter this is to increase your jig weight. As was mentioned in the sea bass chapter, scoping occurs because the boat drifts at a different speed than the current at the bottom, and the drag on your line caused by its resistance in the water causes the line to be pulled away from the boat. This lifts your jig out of the near-bottom strike zone. If the boat was to move at the same speed as the bottom water, your line would hang straight down. In many places wind is usually the main cause of a drifting boat moving at a different speed than the bottom current. At Montauk the currents are complex, and there are times when you have no wind at all yet a 6-ounce jig is required to stay near the bottom due to a significant difference between surface current speed and bottom current speed. Whatever the cause of the scope, you minimize it by using thin and smooth braided line, as was discussed in the sea bass chapter. I jig Montauk with 15-pound-test braid, although 10-pound-test braid is also a good choice and is used by some of the people I fish with. A drift control sock, AKA sea anchor or drogue, will help reduce the wind component of a drift and can allow you to fish lighter weight. As was discussed in an earlier chapter, a trolling motor is the ultimate drift control tool.

I occasionally help Halkias with his charters and I always start by

Cliff Oliver with a fluke that weighed 14.25 pounds bled.

giving clients a main objective – motion in the strike zone. I have superb underwater video showing how fluke will swim right by a drifting strip of fresh meat in order to hit a bouncing bucktail and Gulp rig. They are drawn to motion first, so you need to bounce the rig to get their attention. A large angle in your line will decrease motion on the jig. Try to keep your line near vertical, with a slight angle away from the boat. If you're continuously letting out line to stay down and your rig has scoped out far from the boat, increase the jig weight to reduce the line angle. It's easy to put lots of motion on a 1-ounce jig in shallow water. It's much more challenging with 3- to 6-ounce bucktails in deep water. This is where the choice of bucktail style and rod come into play. I've been fortunate to have others build for me exactly what I want with these two critical pieces of gear.

I've learned a lot by jigging bucktails in the clear water of a swimming pool. One of the more popular bucktail brands that is used for fluke jigging has a fixed hook and a line eye in the middle of the jig so that the jig hangs level. That's great for vertical jigging with a light jig because the level orientation looks natural, and it's easy to bounce a light jig. Try that with progressively heavier jigs and you'll see that by the time you get to 4 ounces, it's tough to put any action at all on the jig. This is especially true with a 6-inch grub tail sticking straight out the back on the fixed hook. The simple reason is that it's very difficult to bounce a large jig up and down with that level orientation. Shift that eye closer to the front of the jig and you'll see that the jigging will produce a sort of dipsy doodle motion. Now change the fixed hook to a swing hook and you'll notice that a nice undulating motion results from the jigging. If you compare the center-eye fixed hook jigging to the forward eye swing hook jigging, you'll see the latter is dancing while the former is barely moving up and down. The S&S Skinner swing-hook fluke bucktails take all of this into account and are made specifically for fluke jigging. Unlike some other heavy bucktails, the hooks on these jigs are sized appropriately for fluke fishing. Because they're swing hooks, they can be changed out easily if desired.

The rod choice is as important as the bucktail style. There are many rods that can bounce a light bucktail, but the taper and power of the rod needs to be considered carefully when fishing heavier jigs and then fighting big fluke on light line. Fast action rods with soft tips will absorb much of your jigging effort instead of transmitting it to the jig. A rod that's too stiff will move the jig, but won't have the spring in it that can help you put action on the jig. A stiff rod also won't cushion the pressure on the line when a big fluke dives for the bottom, which can easily break light line. I prefer rapid jigging, and that becomes difficult to do with rods longer than 7 feet. I find rods a little less than 7 feet to be perfect.

My original ocean fluke rod was a Tsunami Airwave 6.5-footer that was probably out of production before I owned it. I then moved to a Tsunami Classic and a Jigging World Nexus. I trimmed both of those 7-footers by 4 inches, resulting in quite good 6'8" rods. Still, taking a hacksaw to a finished production rod that was designed to function at its original length isn't an ideal thing to do. From those efforts was born the very popular J&H Dark Matter Skinner Jig and Bounce rod. I went through more than a season and four prototypes to get it right, but the result is a 6'8" rod rated for 10- to 30-pound-test line that is perfect for fluke jigging with 1.5- to 6-ounce payloads. The key to its performance is the slower taper as compared to most other rods. When under load, the rod has a parabolic bend utilizing the whole rod, as opposed to only the top half or two-thirds of faster taper rods. Because it bends in the middle, it provides spring that helps bounce the jig. The rod loads beautifully with a fish on, and absorbs those big fluke headshakes that can result in a lost fish if the rod doesn't respond. It was unintentional, but the Jig and Bounce ended up being an excellent all-around rod that became popular for blackfish and general jigging. I use a Quantum Accurist spooled with 15-pound-test braid on this rod when fluke fishing. I use a Maxel Hybrid 20 spooled with 30-pound-test braid for diamond jigging, spoon jigging, and 3-way bucktailing for bass and big bluefish.

I prefer baitcasting to spinning tackle for this fishing. The main reason is that the Quantum Accurist reel that I use has a *Flipping Switch* that allows one to control the reel's clutch with the thumb bar. When the switch is turned on and you press the thumb bar, line is let out. When you release your thumb, the clutch engages. This provides very convenient one-handed depth control as you can let out a little line to stay near the bottom simply by depressing and releasing the thumb bar. If you use spinning gear, you need to reach over with the cranking hand to flip the bail to let out line. That said, there is still a major use for a spinning rod with this fishing.

Many party boat captains alternate their boat's orientation each drift so that anglers on one side of the boat aren't always drifting with their lines running under the boat. If you're on the side of a boat facing down-drift, a spinning rod is an excellent tool to cast in the direction of the drift and then work the jig back until it starts going under the boat, at which time you reel up and repeat the process. There is some advantage to fishing this way because most fish will see your jig before they see the offerings of the anglers on the opposite side of the boat. While I mention party boats for this situation, fishing the "wrong" side of the boat isn't a bad strategy if you're on a rather crowded private boat. A spinning rod for this application should have some of the same properties of the casting rods that I mentioned, and this motivated the development of the spinning version of the Dark Matter Jig and Bounce.

Bottom time – it's the amount of time on any given trip when you're actively fishing your rig. The more time you spend working the strike zone, the better chance you have of catching quality fluke. Two things that cut into this while fishing many hard structure areas are bottom snags and interference fish, especially undersize sea bass. The bottom snags in particular can be very frustrating because quality bucktail rigs aren't cheap, and it takes precious fishing time to re-rig. Avoiding rocky areas will reduce snags, but big fluke love that hard bottom structure because it holds big baits for them to feed on. The best you can do is to try to stay a little off the bottom. Ideally, I'd like to work my rig a foot or two off the bottom, but that's easier said than done since you can't actually see what's going on under the boat. You'll need to occasionally drop down to confirm you're near the bottom. You know your jig has hit bottom when you see momentary float in the line. Keep in mind that if you fish too high, you'll not only be somewhat out of the fluke zone, you're also likely to spend more time dealing with sea bass, which will feed a little higher in the water column than fluke.

If you look at marine charts for areas like Montauk or Block Island, you'll see almost overwhelming structure. Numerous products such as Humminbird Coastmaster and StrikeLines allow for great visualization of bottom contour and structure. An inexpensive way to study structure is to install the Navionics App on your smartphone and turn on *relief shading*. One advantage of the app is that you don't need to be on the boat to view it. I fish on multiple boats that share information with each other, so I find it useful to turn on tracking on my fluke trips so that those tracks can then be pulled up on subsequent trips, regardless of whose boat I'm on. It's easy for me to say that you should look for edges, slopes, and rocky areas when fishing Montauk for fluke, but these are everywhere. A big factor is the confluence of currents, as water flows around Montauk Point to and from Block Island Sound. You need to take this into account because you might have a poor drift in a particular location, but move a few miles to another area, and the water might be flowing fine.

Some areas are well-known and will have several to dozens of boats fishing them on a nice day. Cartwright and Frisbees are two that you're likely to read about in the fishing reports, but even these names refer to general areas. A good strategy is to drift across high spots and along edges and take GPS marks of where you hook up. There are other things to consider as well. The party boats are out every day and these professionals have as good an idea as any of where to fish. However, the last place I want to set a drift is where a party boat is fishing. Imagine a fluke inclined to eat something, and along comes a party boat with 30 or more offerings of varying types and presentations. I bet that fluke hops on a rig! Those are big boats that paint with a wide brush. It pays to keep your distance from them. On a smaller scale, don't stop directly up drift of another boat, else you may end up covering the same water they just did. In terms of etiquette, don't ever set up in the path of where someone else is drifting. This is called "short drifting" and you'll make instant enemies on the water if you do this.

The best day I've ever had fishing Montauk was also the most crowded. It's no exaggeration that there were at least a hundred boats at Cartwright, and I have the video posted on my YouTube channel to prove it. Halkias was piloting his 25-ft Cobia and we were fishing with Michael Kim from Tackle World, and John's friend, Tony. The four of us had a ridiculously good day that included Halkias pausing to reel in a 9-pounder while he watched Michael Kim scoop up my 12-plus pounder, which was my 12th keeper of the trip. We were barely recovered from that fish when Tony boated an 8-pounder. Halkias used a single strategy the entire day – just pick an open lane. As best as possible, he avoided repeating anyone's drift. It worked, as we bailed fish the whole trip.

Should we stay or move? It's the question on everyone's mind during anything but a solid bite. There's a feature of Montauk fishing that I

A 12-pound-plus fluke that I caught and released on a wild Montauk trip in 2018.

have not experienced to the same extent while fishing other areas. I find it much more spurty. It's not uncommon to grind for hours catching just an occasional fish, only to have it turn on to the point where there's almost always someone on the boat with a fish on. These spurts seem to last around 90 minutes, and are almost certainly current-related. You would think these could be timed by adding roughly an hour to the previous day's good fishing window, but it rarely works that way. While tides are predictable, winds and water conditions can alter currents, and this likely contributes to the inconsistency. If we experience a good bite for a while, but it shuts down, we're likely to stay and hope it turns on again. None of this is an exact science, but if we caught a bunch of fish and they stopped hitting, they're almost certainly still there, and knowing where the fish are is half the battle.

Fish are usually concentrated in small areas. This goes for fluke fishing in general, but when you hook up multiple times around a

Jack Breese with a 14.65-pound fluke.

particular spot, shorten your drift and pound that spot. As mentioned, the good bites don't usually last very long, and it pays to maximize the time spent fishing small hotspots. Unless you're really searching, long drifts rarely make sense. This goes for all types of fishing.

There are times when I'm pretty sure you could drop a hot dog down on a rope and a fluke would hit it. This is one of the things I think holds many anglers back from becoming more productive with fluke. "This is how we always catch them," is a frequent defense of anglers who are set in their ways and are unwilling to try new things. In the overall history of ocean fluke fishing, light tackle jigging is still a relatively new technique. If you're not yet converted, give it a try. Few people who do ever go back to dragging bait.

Rick Kohut with a Montauk doormat Fluke.

CHAPTER 21
BIG SPOONS – BIG BASS

"That's stupid," I thought to myself as I watched John Halkias tie a giant spoon lure to his line with the intention of dropping it to the bottom 90 feet below. "I don't think you're gonna get down," I offered, as he defended the test by saying the current had slowed. "Slow" was a relative term here, as the current was actually moving at over 2 mph. That's considered pretty fast in most places, but this was Plum Gut, the small canyon of water between the eastern tip of Long Island's North Fork and Plum Island. Currents here run between 3 and 5 mph in the middle of the tide. It's one of the most challenging places to fish in the Northeast because the bottom rises and falls rapidly in the fishable depth range of about 20 to 100 feet. That wouldn't be so bad if it wasn't for the very rocky bottom that holds decades worth of lost fishing gear to get snagged on.

The standard method of fishing *The Gut* involves a three-way rig with a roughly 6-foot leader of 80-pound-test line to a bucktail, and a one-foot length of lighter line to an 8- to 20-ounce sinker. The main line of at least 30-pound-test braid is connected to the remaining loop of the 3-way swivel. The bucktail weighs only around 1 ¼ ounces, as it's the heavy sinker that gets and keeps you in the near-bottom strike zone. You drop this to the bottom, reel up a couple of cranks, and then try to follow the bottom contour as you drift quickly up and down big slopes. If you drag bottom, you are very likely to snag and break off. The line that attaches the sinker to the rig is lighter than the main line and the bucktail leader so that if you snag the sinker, you might be able to sacrifice it to save the rest of the rig. Historically a lot of big striped bass are caught in Plum

Gut, but recent years have seen most of the daytime fish weighing less than 15 pounds. Decades ago when the regulations were more lax, hook and line commercial fishermen, AKA pinhookers, could make a pretty good living there catching stripers for market.

I'm not sure when it happened, but sometime in the preceding couple of seasons very large flutter spoons started becoming popular for striped bass fishing. We saw them used with amazing success one morning around a month earlier in the Jessup's rips of Peconic Bay. I was on John's boat that morning as well, and we both knew the anglers who were beating up on the bass with giant spoons while most of the rest of the fleet caught predominantly bluefish. We learned they were using 8-inch 3.5-ounce Ben Parker Nichols Spoons. The spoons apparently had their origins in Largemouth Bass fishing in lakes where the primary forage was large shad. The spoons eventually made their way to the saltwater striper environment and the hardware was modified to stand up to the salt. The spoon that John was tying on was one of the Nichols Spoons with hardware meant for big saltwater stripers.

I was already convinced that these spoons worked great on stripers, having seen them catch at Jessup's and then learning that they were popular in the 10- to 40-foot depths of Raritan Bay, which often holds a lot of adult bunker that the stripers key on. My negative reaction to John trying one in the Gut was that I couldn't understand how it would ever make it to the bottom and then stay in the near-bottom strike zone, given that we both needed at least 10-ounce sinkers to keep our bucktail rigs down.

I was surprised to hear John announce "I hit bottom" on his first drift, but I was intrigued when I saw him lean back on a fish. Unfortunately, that fish never made it to the surface, as the line parted mysteriously. He boated only one of three hookups in his short experiment, and although it was a bluefish that might have hit higher in the water column, he did prove that he could get the spoon to the bottom and keep it in the strike zone.

A few days later, John was at my house with a generous supply of Tony Maja spoons. Maja might be best known for his bunker spoons, but these were what he called *Drift Spoons*. These 9-inch 5-ounce spoons in solid white and solid chartreuse went right into my tackle bag, and would be first in the water for me the following morning on Rick Kohut's 32-foot Metal Shark *Blu-J*.

We had our usual 4-person fluke crew on board, which included Cliff and Jack, anglers who both boated fluke in excess of 14 pounds on Rick's boat in previous seasons. We were fishing bass this particular morning because the Montauk fluke fishing had been slow while the nearby Gut bassing had been excellent. Running 18 miles round-trip for steady rod bending with stripers sounded like a lot more fun than running 70 miles for a fluke grind.

Everyone on board was experienced in fishing the Gut. Cliff started with a 3-way bucktail rig, while Jack used a simpler rig consisting of only a 6-ounce bucktail. Both had pork rind or similar strips on their jigs. Excited to have experienced bucktailers to compare against, I started with the 9-inch spoon as an experiment. My rig was simple, with a 5-foot leader of 80-pound-test Fluorocarbon connected to the main line through a high-quality barrel swivel and tied direct to the spoon.

Rick, who stayed on the wheel and never even wet a line this trip, stopped the boat in about 100 feet of water. As this was early in the tide, the drift speed was still less than 3 mph, but that was plenty fast to move us up the slope with good jig presentations. I hesitated to put down at first, opting to wait until we were in the 80-foot range because I had no confidence in getting to the bottom in deeper water. The sight of Cliff leaning back on a good fish changed my mind, and I dropped the spoon while still in 95 feet. There was a slight breeze against the current, so we were fishing the down drift side of the boat and my spoon began scoping out in the direction we were drifting. I paid close attention to the line, but couldn't detect my spoon hitting bottom. When I let out what I felt was probably too much line, I engaged the reel and began a series of skyward rod sweeps letting the spoon fall in between. As I did this the line angle began decreasing. Aware that we would soon be in less than 60 feet of water and I'd risk losing the spoon if I dragged and snagged bottom, I started recovering some line between rod sweeps.

Two minutes into what would be at most a four-minute drift, I really had no clue where the spoon was. Cliff lost his fish, but the fact that he had hooked one while I couldn't even figure out where my lure was had me planning to ditch the spoon on the next drift. "This is silly," I said as I took a few cranks to retrieve the spoon. The thought was interrupted by a brief hookup, and as I laughed about having actually hooked something with the wayward spoon, my rod was yanked down hard on the next lift. "No thanks to my technique!" I announced, as the 25-pounder hit the deck a couple of minutes later. Jack, who had been fishing the Gut frequently in recent weeks, looked at the fish and said they hadn't caught any that big. The spoon obviously earned a second drop.

This time I actually detected bottom, at which point I began a series of upward sweeps and drops while watching the line for slack indicating a bottom collision or fish. My rod stopped short on one of the upward sweeps, and I soon had another good bass on the deck. The spoon produced 4 more fish in the 25- to 30-pound range on the next 5 drifts. The drift that I didn't catch on was cut short because I hung bottom and we ran up-current to free the spoon. I was hooked up for most of the trip while my boatmates caught next to nothing on the standard bucktail rigs. Rick commented that the nearby boats were not catching anything in numbers or size like I was. I didn't notice, as I was busy almost all of the time. Two days later I proved it wasn't just luck as I used four different spoons from both Maja and Nichols in three different colors and caught on all of them. My biggest was a 40-pounder on an 8-inch Nichols spoon, which was an exceptional catch for 11 a.m. in the Gut.

More out of luck than anything else, the Dark Matter Skinner Jig and Bounce "Fluke Rod" turned out to be ideal for spoon jigging. Its slower taper that allows bend in the middle of the rod provides the spring to help lift the spoon effortlessly, while the straight section of the rod ahead of the handle provides the power to easily handle big fish in current. The difference between fluke fishing and bass fishing the rips with this rod is in the reel and line used. When fluke fishing I use a low profile baitcaster spooled with 15-pound-test braid, but I replace that with something like a Maxel Hybrid 25 or Penn Squall 15 spooled with 30-pound braid when striper fishing. I was already using these rods for 3-way bucktailing in the Gut, so the only change for spoon fishing was to replace the three-way rig with the previously mentioned leader tied direct to a spoon.

The four of us on that first trip had well over a combined 100 years of at least occasional Plum Gut fishing experience. We were blown away that any artificial could heavily out-fish in numbers and size the traditional offerings refined over decades to work under the challenging constraints imposed by those waters. None of us could understand how the spoon could get to and stay in the near-bottom strike zone. That trip is linked to the QR code in this chapter so you can watch for yourself. I get a lot of comments on my YouTube videos, and several suggested thumbing the spool lightly on the drop to keep the spoon from fluttering slowly to the bottom. In looking back at the video, I think the line belly and current in the Gut put enough tension on the line to orient the spoon vertically, causing it to slice its way through the water column rather quickly to get to the bottom. On a Long Island Sound trip the following week, I made a couple of test drops with the spoon while thumbing the spool lightly, and that approach did indeed keep the spoon slicing to the bottom instead of fluttering.

This book was actually finished and ready to go to layout when I interrupted the process to add this chapter. While I would not normally devote book space to a lure I had used on only two trips, it was exactly my inexperience that made the lure's productivity so striking. I had no idea what I was doing, didn't even have a good feel for where the spoon was on the initial drift, but still managed six big bass on my first seven drops.

Rick Kohut fighting a big bass that hit a spoon in Plum Gut.

I added this chapter late in the process for two reasons. First, I wanted to bring the big spoons to the attention of readers who had never tried one and impress upon them that apparently no prior experience is required to make these lures work. More importantly, I felt the incredible productivity of this lure that was relatively new to the environment I tested it in raised an important question: What else are we not thinking about? Spoons are probably among the first lures ever made, yet I'm comfortable in saying that giant drift spoons were relatively new to striper fishing in many areas as I wrote this book. Are there other lure types, perhaps used in unrelated fisheries, that could change the way we target certain species? You can bet I'll be taking those big spoons to Florida to drop around the reefs.

The biggest reason that I see anglers not catch to their full potential is that they make the assumption that because they've caught in the past with a particular technique or offering, that they must be fishing correctly. Catching some fish should never be used as evidence that your approach is the most productive. The best example I see of this is in the fluke fishery where some people still drag squid and spearing on the bottom because that's the way they've always done it and they've caught lots of fluke that way. If these anglers tried targeting fluke with jigs on lighter tackle, it's extremely unlikely they'd go back to bait. In a million years I never would have believed that any lure could out-fish a 3-way bucktail rig or heavy bucktail while drift fishing Plum Gut, but my flutter spoon experience has me re-evaluating that, and approaches to other fisheries as well.

A 40-pound striper that hit an 8-inch Nichols Flutter Spoon in Plum Gut.

CHAPTER 22

MY 50 YEARS ON THE EDGE AND SOME PARTING ADVICE

My earliest memories of life were of bottom fishing with worms while my parents socialized with friends on their 26-ft Owens Cabin Cruiser. Most Friday evenings in the summer we would go to the boat docked in Port Jefferson Harbor and cruise with several other boats to the Narrows of Conscience Bay, about a mile from the marina. Our family of five, of which I was the youngest, would spend the weekends there. Imagine having to entertain such a young child on a 26-ft boat for two days and nights! What could you possibly do to occupy the little one? In my case the answer was to have lots of sandworms. The flounder and blowfish would take care of the rest. This activity went on from when I was first old enough to hold a fishing rod until I was seven years old, at which time my younger brother's arrival forced the sale of the boat.

In the final summer before it all came to an end, I was old enough to do all of the aspects of the fishing myself, including baiting hooks and releasing fish. There was one rule that I needed to follow – do not use the big worms. Those were reserved for my father and older brother who would troll them along the shore on homemade spinner lures behind our little red 1948 Penn Yan dinghy powered by a temperamental 3 ½-hp McCulloch outboard. Sometimes they would return to the mother ship with one or two fish of a kind that I had never caught before. They had stripes.

There was a silver lining in the sale of the big boat, in that some of the proceeds were used to buy a new 1968 13-ft Boston Whaler. This relatively speedy craft with its 18 hp Evinrude could get to Conscience Bay from the marina in a few minutes, and unlike the little dinghy, there was room for me. I needed only to let the line out until I was told to stop, then engage the bail on the green spinning reel and hold on tight. "Bump" was usually the two-second warning before the tip of the rod was pulled hard toward the stern of the boat. For some reason the fish always seemed to tap the spinner first, before trying to eat it. The striped fish were hooked this way, and so was I.

We moved to a new home in Miller Place when I was ten. At the end of the street was a tall set of 184 steps that led to the beach on the edge of Long Island Sound. The striped fish were there too, and given that this was a different time, I could walk to the beach by myself and try to catch them anytime I wanted. Worms were no longer needed, as a shiny Hopkins lure often caught the fish I now knew as striped bass. The three lures I would bring to the beach in a pencil case soon grew into a whole bag of various lures that I wore over my shoulder. I knew all of the lure names and became consumed with understanding which ones to use and when. When a grammar school teacher asked our class if anyone knew what an atom was, my hand shot up quickly. "*It's a popping plug - white with a blue head!*" I had a hard time accepting that my answer wasn't what she was looking for. Fishing was already progressing from something I did occasionally for fun, to an obsession that creeped into other aspects of life.

My wife of nearly forty years, Kim, understood what she was getting into well in advance of our wedding day, and that she would have to recalibrate her definition of normal behavior. She learned that lesson late one April night in 1984. This was the beginning of my graduate school days near the shore of Lake Ontario. There was a serious fishery there with trout into the teens and salmon into the 30-pound-class. Unfortunately, I had few lures appropriate for that kind of fishing and little money to stock up properly. One of the places I fished with my limited supply of spoons was a 400-ft long fishing pier a little east of Rochester. Although I didn't lose many lures there, I frequently saw others snag bottom and break off with the light monofilament line of the time. On a mid-April Saturday morning of my first year there, I was shocked to see the pier packed with people on my arrival for some fishing. It was then that I heard about the Empire State Lake Ontario (ESLO) Trout and Salmon Derby. I would learn later that upwards of 15,000 anglers participated in the weekend-long contest every April. I didn't bother fishing the pier that morning, as there was no room, but I watched for a while as lure after lure was claimed by the bottom. It was then that knew how I was going to build a Lake Ontario lure arsenal for free.

Among the things I brought North with me was snorkeling gear. Water temperatures were generally in the low to mid forties in the lake, but I reasoned that they would be at the upper end of that range late in the day along the shore. This would be tolerable in my Farmer John wetsuit. A complication was that the park was fished until dark, and swimming was prohibited. For reasons I don't recall, my diving gear included a dive light. My plan was to slip into the water after dark, and clean all of those lost lures from the bottom. As someone who had dove for lures in Long Island Sound since a young teen, and later dove for lobsters at night, this seemed like absolutely normal behavior. Sunset wasn't until around 8 p.m., so there was no sense in getting to the park before 9 p.m. Kim and I were dating at this point, and I mentioned to her during the day that I was heading to the pier to dive for lures that night.

There were still people milling around when I got there, so I didn't suit up until the park cleared out around 9:30 p.m. When I slipped into three feet of water from the little wall that borders the lake, I couldn't imagine that I'd be able to tolerate full submersion in the cold dark water. I had come this far though, so I would have to try. It took about 15 minutes to gradually acclimate myself to the point that I could slip beneath the surface with the spotlight and mesh lobster bag in my left hand, and my other hand free to pick up lures. As my light beam reached the bottom on my first breath, it was immediately reflected back by multiple scattered lures. I grabbed three on my first submersion, and forgot all about the cold. It was now nearly 10 p.m., and given that the wall and pier that met at a right angle were each over 400 feet long, there was a lot of bottom to cover.

Unlike the life-filled water I was accustomed to on Long Island, this was dead water over a brown rocky bottom. The only exception being a few 20- to 40-pound class carp that startled the crap out of me each time one would show up in my light beam. I was busy and had no concern about the passage of time as I went back and forth progressively farther into the lake while trying not to overlap my previous passes. Most breaths yielded lures, many of which looked like they just came off a tackle shop wall. There was no time for inspection, as I did my best to get them into the bottom of my bag without tangling the hooks on the mesh on the way in. I'd sort it all out when I got back to my apartment.

Unbeknownst to me, Kim wasn't having as good a night as I was. As the hour grew later, and my car didn't reappear at the apartment building, she began to worry. From my perspective, my night was a refreshing reminder of normal Long Island behavior. But from the perspective of a girl from the middle of Upstate New York, my being out past midnight when I said I was going to the park to dive for lures was alarming to say the least. Things were only going to get scarier for her, as she woke up a friend and the two girls headed for the lake-side park in the middle of the night. They arrived to find my car by itself in the parking lot. It's clear to me now that someone not completely familiar with my range of water-related activities could draw only one conclusion from this – John drowned.

When I came up for a breath and saw flashlights in the distance heading in my direction, I immediately killed my light. In my mind these were cops, and I was in the park after hours, swimming no less. The fines could easily surpass all of the lure money I had just saved. Then I heard the crying, and realizing what was happening, turned my light back on. "What's going on?" I asked, as if I didn't know. Confusion, relief, and tinge of anger came together as she pleaded for me to get out of the water. "Okay, ten more lures and I'm out." Then I actually proceeded to dive for a few more minutes until I added ten more lures to the bag. The final take for the night was 113 lures. In retrospect, I should have explained my night's plans to her in more detail. She got over it in the end, and we married the following year. The mid-October wedding date was chosen carefully to fall in a fishing lull between the salmon and steelhead runs.

Sadly, my worst transgression as far as Kim was concerned was yet to come. When our first child, Katie, was born, there were complications and she went immediately to Stony Brook's Pediatric ICU. They never

Kim Skinner with a nice fluke caught in Long Island Sound.

moved her to the regular nursery, but instead discharged her directly from ICU to our care four days after she was born. As far as I could tell, the discharge time was chosen with total disregard for the fact that there was a low water turn right around the time we were to pick up our new baby. This was April 27, which going all the way back to when I was 13 years old, had been a day I associated with good fishing and the first stripers of the season. Within an hour of arriving home, I left the new mother and baby alone, while I caught the incoming tide and my first three stripers of the season. My wife and I were married seven years at that point, and she didn't even give me a hard time about it. As parenthood sunk in however, I understood what I had done.

Fortunately for everyone involved, becoming a parent caused me to quickly adjust my priorities, and I can say with confidence that neither my wife nor my two children would ever say that I put fishing ahead of the family after that one incident. With the best striper fishing being in the middle of the night, I simply shifted my fishing focus to the hours when everyone else slept.

Suffice it to say that fishing has been a major part of my life since my earliest memories. There have been times when I focused intensely on a single species, but it's been the diversification into different species and environments that I've found the most rewarding and enlightening. More than a dozen species of saltwater fish from the Northeast to Florida found their way into the pages of this book, without even mentioning the freshwater bass, pike, trout, and salmon of my years in the Lake Ontario region. Looking back at fifty-plus years of trying to keep a bend in the rod, there are a few key pieces of advice I'll leave you with.

Unless you are very experienced with a particular fishery and fishing spot, stick to a small handful of proven offerings. The objective is to reduce the number of variables, and one of the biggest unknowns is whether or not a fish will respond to the lure you're presenting. Even with all of the years of experience that I have fishing for stripers on Long Island Sound beaches, you are likely to be underwhelmed if you look into my daytime surf bag where you'll find only pencil poppers, spooks, and bucktails.

I take the same approach with my Southwest Florida fishery, which was still relatively new to me as I wrote this. Most of my fishing there is done with either a small spook plug or a 5-inch Gulp Jerk Shad on a swimbait hook. The snook, redfish, and trout that I target all hit the spook, although sometimes they're less likely to hit topwater in the middle of the day. If the fish are willing to hit any lure at all, there's a good chance they'll hit the jerk shad. With my spooks and jerk shads, I'm confident that I'm offering extremely productive lures, so that's one less thing to think about as I search for fish along the endless mangrove shorelines. That leads me to the next piece of advice – apply what you have learned from one fishery into a new fishery that you're trying to learn.

As I approached my first attempts of catching Southern fish, I kept reverting to thinking like a striper fisherman. In the end, all fish are just trying to acquire more energy than they expend. This translates to leveraging the effects of current, and using it to put baitfish in a position where they can be consumed with minimal effort. While knowledge transfer from a fishery you're familiar with will jumpstart efforts into a new fishery, you still must do your homework. In fishing Florida I've had to study the impacts that temperature changes and wind have on a shallow water fishery with temperature-sensitive species such as snook. My striper experience didn't help much with that, but regional fishing publications have.

Subscribe to and read publications that cover fisheries you're interested in. I subscribe to the *Fisherman* and *On the Water* up North. Given my experience level there, a lot of the material is stuff I already know and I read only a small percentage of articles, but I still learn things! In my Southern fishery, I subscribe to *Florida Sport Fishing* and *Florida Sportsman*. It takes me some time to get through each issue of those because I have so much to learn. Fishing books are particularly valuable because I can state from experience that there is a lot of pressure on the author to turn out a good product. The fact that you're reading this tells me you probably don't need much convincing regarding the value of books dedicated to fishing.

While I suggest that you read as much as you can on your fisheries, I'll urge you to not take accepted norms as gospel. As mentioned in Chapter 20, I was told over and over again that light tackle bucktailing for fluke wouldn't work in deep ocean water and that bucktails and Gulp wouldn't out-fish real bait. I probably have fifty videos on my

YouTube channel to the contrary. I read frequently in regional Florida publications that snook don't feed well until the water temperature is above 70 degrees, and that topwater is a poor choice in the cooler water. My best fishing for large snook has all occurred in water less than 65 degrees, and most of that has been on topwater early in the morning when the water was its coolest of the day. In the years I lived in Riverhead Town, I caught many bass in the 30- to 45-pound class from those beaches where most people considered a 20-pounder a big fish. The cows were there, and probably still are, but you would never know if you didn't fish the area with live and rigged eels at night and big pencil poppers at dusk and dawn. Before I found those fish, I spent 19 seasons quietly catching large stripers farther east on the "wrong tide." While it's important to take in available information, it pays to think outside the box. You'll fail most of the time, but you'll find undiscovered strategies too.

"Bump." We'll end where we started, with that tap on the end of the rod that signals we did something right, or maybe just got lucky. Few pursuits in life can provide the lifelong challenges and rewards of fishing, whether we're refining skills on a familiar fishery, or enjoying small victories on a new fishery as if every catch was a trophy. My fifty plus years of fishing has taught me that neither the target species nor circumstance matters, as it's the endless possibilities of what that bump might lead to that quickens the pulse and draws us to the water.

OTHER BOOKS WRITTEN BY
JOHN SKINNER

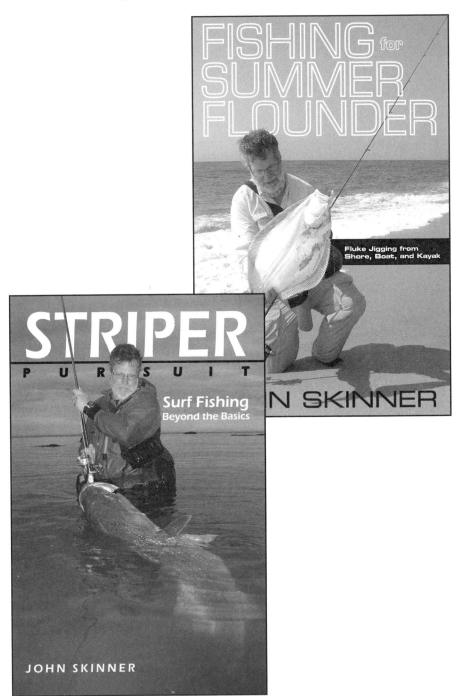

OTHER BOOKS WRITTEN BY JOHN SKINNER